THE ESSENCE OF TRAGEDY

DAVID IRVIN

© David Irvin 2015

All rights reserved

No part of this publication may be reproduced, stored in a retrieval system, or transmitted in any form or by any means, without the prior permission in writing of the publisher, nor be otherwise circulated in any form of binding or cover other than that in which it is published and without a similar condition including this condition being imposed on the subsequent purchaser.

All paper used in the printing of this book has been made from wood grown in managed, sustainable forests.

ISBN 978-1-78003-864-3

Printed and published in the UK

Author Essentials Ltd
4 The Courtyard
South Street
Falmer
BN1 9PQ

A catalogue record of this book is available from the British Library

Cover design by Jacqueline Abromeit

There's a divinity that shapes our ends
Rough-hew them how we will

                        Shakespeare: *Hamlet*

I am the master of my fate
I am the captain of my soul

                William Ernest Henley: *Invictus*

CONTENTS

INTRODUCTION 1

Aeschylus: *The Oresteian Trilogy* 5

Sophocles: *The Theban Plays* 15

Euripides, Seneca, Racine: *Phaedra Plays* 25

Christopher Marlowe: *Doctor Faustus* 36

Shakespeare: *Hamlet, King Lear, Othello, Macbeth* 44

Jacobean and Caroline Theatre 1603–1642: 59
John Webster: *The Duchess of Malfi*
John Ford: *'Tis Pity She's a Whore*

John Milton: *Samson Agonistes* 69

Verdi: *Rigoletto* 78

Thomas Hardy: *The Mayor of Casterbridge* 85

August Strindberg: *Miss Julie* 93

Henrik Ibsen: *Hedda Gabler* and *The Master Builder* 103

Anton Chekhov: *The Seagull* 114

George Bernard Shaw: *Saint Joan* 122

Eugene O'Neill: *Mourning Becomes Electra* 130

T.S. Eliot: *Murder in the Cathedral* 140

Bertolt Brecht: *Mother Courage and her Children* 149

Tennessee Williams: *A Streetcar Named Desire* 158

Arthur Miller: *Death of a Salesman* 166

The Death of Tragedy 175

Jesus Of Nazareth 182

APPENDICES 187

INTRODUCTION

I have no doubt that tragic theatre is the highest art form, capable of taking us to the heights of ecstatic insight and the depths of suicidal depression. Of course music and dance can provide similar life enhancement but theatrical drama is expressed in words, and words afford all kinds of nuances and, in addition, give a permanence to the drama, rendering it capable of both analysis and recall.

In this series of essays I want to explore a number of the best known tragedies, to some extent putting them into their historical context, but essentially showing their relevance today as a potential source of personal insight and eternal wisdom. For the most part it will be plays that are discussed but I will also discuss an opera (Verdi's *Rigoletto*) and a novel (Hardy's *The Mayor of Casterbridge*) and I will conclude with the story of Jesus of Nazareth.

For all of these dramas have one thing in common, which is the downfall of someone who has enjoyed stature or pre-eminence, thus making their fall so much more spectacular and noteworthy – and their learning through this process so much more incisive and profound. In this context, of course, Aristotle who, in his *Poetics*, set down classical theories of tragedy warrants a mention. Although I shall be following my own theory as to the nature of tragedy, I will make references to a number of factors discussed by Aristotle.

The word tragedy means a goat song and involved the ritual sacrifice of a goat to song and dance. The singing and dancing evolved to the Chorus in Greek plays, and the goat became a human. What is important for us, though, about Aristotle's formulation of, as he saw it, the rules which should govern tragedy is that the tragic hero should be someone of some greatness who falls from this height of greatness by a reversal in his fortunes as a result of an error[1] (**not** as a result of any intervention by the gods or fate or bad luck or society). As we shall see more fully Arthur Miller in the twentieth century made a case both in theory and on stage for an ordinary person to be the central tragic figure.

Aristotle spoke of catharsis, the purging of emotions, particularly those of pity and fear, whereby the audience leaves the theatre drained. I think tragedy does more than this. I see tragic heroes as representatives of humanity and they suffer on behalf of every man, so that their self-knowledge and understanding of the world, which they gain as they descend into their personal abyss, becomes a template for the knowledge we all gain through suffering.[2] They are writ larger than we are and their suffering is for the most part much greater but we can identify with the nature of their experience and learn from it vis-à-vis self-knowledge and awareness and ultimate coming to terms with the nature of being human in an apparently callous world.

I think *Hamlet* is a good example of that. Hamlet's father is murdered and his mother marries his father's murderer (who also happens to be his father's brother, Hamlet's uncle). That is extreme and, as far as I am aware, happens rarely. But it is a common experience for a child to lose a father and for the widowed mother then to marry someone deemed totally unsuitable by that child. Showing dissatisfaction by killing the new husband is an extreme option, most unlikely to be taken, but the anguish felt at the sudden death of one's father and one's mother then making a hasty and disapproved of marriage is something that many people have to contend with: initially the coming to terms with grief and then the adjustment to a new unexpected family member enjoying intimacy with your mother. It's not easy. We can identify with Hamlet's feelings and this helps us explore ours. I see the tragic hero as a Super Representative of mankind.

Hegel[3] too had a theory of tragedy, in which he contrasts Greek with Shakespearean tragedy. Acknowledging the individuality of the Greek heroes he nonetheless sees them as involved in a conflict with ethical forces, whereas the Shakespearean tragic hero "decides in accordance with subjective desires". This is clarified when, referring to Hamlet, Hegel writes: "in Hamlet's soul, we understand that death has lurked from the beginning... we feel he is a man whom inner disgust has almost consumed well before death comes upon him from the outside."

I don't want to get bogged down in academic theories about tragedy, but there will inevitably be some reference to Aristotle and Miller and Hegel throughout the following series of essays. As there will be too to Nietzsche, whose view of the potential exalting power of tragedy is much closer to my own. Nietzsche[4] argued that Socrates had potentially killed tragedy by his emphasis on reason as the tool to unlock the mysteries of existence. Nietzsche would have none of this. Of course reason is needed to construct a play, but the force that energises a play is a sensual force, which accepts the terrors of reality and fate, and Nietzsche sees this as a Yes-saying force. In his book *Twilight of the Idols* Nietzsche writes: "Saying Yes to life even in its strangest and most painful episodes, the will to life rejoicing in its own inexhaustible vitality even as it witnesses the destruction of its greatest heroes – that is what I call Dionysian[5] …Not in order to be liberated from terror and pity, not in order to purge oneself of a dangerous affect by its vehement discharge – which is how Aristotle understood tragedy – but in order to celebrate oneself the eternal joy of becoming, beyond all terror and pity – that tragic joy included even joy in destruction."

So for Nietzsche tragedy can be exhilarating – in *Twilight of the Idols* he writes of "an overflowing feeling of life and strength, where even pain still has the effect of a stimulus". As well as seeing tragic heroes as Super Representatives from whom we can all gain insight and understanding, I see tragedy similarly to Nietzsche. It is not escapist and does not pull punches. It tackles the major issues of life and meaning and it does this, not through arid philosophical discussion, but through confronting directly the human experience of life and death. As such it can be dynamic and vitalising – but it can also lead to what Kurtz discovered in Conrad's *The Heart of Darkness*, that is "the horror, the horror."

It is time to explore all these life and death and meaning issues through some of the greatest plays ever written. Too much theory! The play's the thing!

---

[1] The Greek word for this is *hamartia*, once translated as "a fatal flaw" (in the hero's character) but now recognised as more correctly rendered as "a mistake or error."

Continued…

2. Aeschylus: "Wisdom comes alone through suffering."
   Dostoevsky: "Suffering is the sole origin of consciousness."

3. in *The Phenomenology of Spirit*

4. in *The Birth of Tragedy*

5. Nietzsche writes at length about the two complementary strains in Greek culture – the Apollonian and the Dionysian. The Apollonian factor is rational, giving shape and order to the Dionysian impulses which are mystical and spiritual which can both intoxicate and plumb the depths of horror and despair.

AESCHYLUS: *The Oresteian Trilogy*

From the Lion Gate at Mycenae, looking across the flat miles of the Argos plain, the triumphal return journey of Agamemnon had been visible for hours. His queen Clytemnestra and her lover Aegisthus had so much time to plan their welcome. Agamemnon was fresh from the ultimately successful 10-year siege of Troy and he had with him, as concubine, the captured Trojan princess Cassandra. In fact the kind of welcome Agamemnon was to receive had almost certainly been planned ten years previously: that was when, a fleet having been assembled in order to attack Troy and bring back the abducted Helen from the arms of Paris, the wind refused to fill the sails of the fleet and they were all battered by northern gales in the harbour of Aulis. Agamemnon responded to the prophet Calchas's dictum that the sacrifice of Agamemnon's daughter Iphigenia would bring about a shift in wind direction. Other, much less drastic sacrifices, having failed, Agamemnon reluctantly agrees and sends for his daughter on the pretext, believed by his wife and daughter, that he has arranged for Iphigenia to be married to Achilles. Iphigenia is killed and the wind changes. And Clytemnestra, sister to Helen but now more powerfully motivated by the loss of her daughter, waits for the opportunity to avenge Iphigenia. She has waited ten years; the beacons along the coast signalling the fall of Troy have been lit and now Agamemnon is making his triumphal progress towards her.

This is all explained by the Chorus at the beginning of the first play in the trilogy, *Agamemnon*, and it is spelt out that: "The killer will be killed." Clytemnestra, though, publicly expresses her delight that her husband is coming home: "Argos longs for him" and claims that Agamemnon "will find at home a wife as faithful as he left", that she has found no pleasure with other men and there is not a whiff of scandal around her. A Herald, who has been in Troy and had previously spoken of the unpleasant fighting conditions the Greek army had had to endure, is sceptical of the queen's statements but the Chorus comments: "A very proper statement – unimpeachable!"

Clytemnestra welcomes her husband and a path of crimson cloth is spread from his chariot to the palace door. She also welcomes Cassandra. Cassandra, though, adds to the "foreboding hour" felt by the Chorus: she has already gained a reputation as a prophet and a doom-sayer, and here she foresees the conspiracy and the hunting-net (which is to be used in the killing of Agamemnon). She has seen through Clytemnestra's brazen "superb bluff": "There is a smell of murder. The walls drip with blood." She knows her own hour is come too. And, true enough, Clytemnestra, having wrapped Agamemnon in a hunting-net, stabs him three times while in the bath and kills him and then Cassandra. The people of Argos are unhappy about this and see the continuation of the story through Agamemnon (and Clytemnestra's) son having to avenge his father's death (foreseen too by Cassandra). Clytemnestra justifies her behaviour with "the sinner dies"; Aegisthus threatens the critical Chorus and the play concludes with Clytemnestra saying: "You and I, joint rulers, will enforce due reverence for our throne." This marks the end of the working out of the curse on their family, the House of Atreus, which goes back for two generations.

Of course there are all kinds of moral issues to do with personal responsibility, the morality of revenge, the parts played by the gods or Fate, the achievement of justice in society, but before we look at these, it is important that I explain why I have begun these series of essays with Aeschylus's *Agamemnon*. Quite simply, it is the historical context.

The plays of Aeschylus (525–456 BC) are the earliest surviving Greek (Athenian) tragedies. Indeed although we know that tragedy as drama dates back to the sixth century BC, we have no plays from then, and of the thousand plus plays written in the fifth century just thirty-two survived – and only the plays of Aeschylus, Sophocles and Euripides remain intact. I think all these survivors are pretty remarkable: it makes one wonder what we have missed...

Festival time for the Athenians was springtime – on the cusp of April. The celebration was in honour of Dionysus, the god of fertility and wine and the loosening of inhibitions, which leads him to also being the god of creativity and poetry. Originally three playwrights competed in the festival over three successive days, each presenting three tragedies and concluding with a comedy, known as a satyr. The stories of the plays could be linked but not necessarily: Aeschylus's *Oresteia* is the sole trilogy that has survived. The plays were enacted in the open air, the citizens were encouraged to attend and those who could not afford the price of admission were subsidised in full by the state. Four plays probably meant such festivals were all-day events. Wagner's *Parsifal* and a full text production of *Hamlet* take a chunk out of any audience's life, but this was more like Wagner's *Ring Cycle*. Perhaps a better analogy would be to liken it all to a Test Match. Large theatres like that of Dionysus in Athens could hold an audience of 12,000. Altars to the gods and priests – and, I suspect, fast food stalls – were everywhere. It was all a wonderful day-out for the community, very socially cohesive and encouraged by the local governments.

As far as we can tell most of the content of the plays was taken from Homer[1], with the serious issues of the survival of heroes of legend and history beset, as they were, by all kind of either self or god-induced trials and tribulations at its centre. At the time of Aeschylus's writing Athens, having expelled its last tyrant in 510 BC, was in the full flush of a belief in democracy: all citizens – by majority voting – were involved in determining judicial and political matters. So matters of justice and vengeance and Fate were at the forefront of the minds of citizens in a functioning democracy. The Dionysian spring drama festivals made an outstanding contribution to the debate about and understanding of these issues.

The features of Greek tragic stage presentation were that all actors were male and wore masks; plays were composed in metrical form and the Chorus danced as well as sang their rhythmic metres. There were one or two interesting stage devices too: the use of a crane whereby a god/goddess could make a flying entrance, giving us the expression "deus ex machina"; and the *ekkylema*, a platform hidden until it is appropriate to reveal (usually) the result of some violent off-stage action – the disclosure of the butchered bodies of Agamemnon and Cassandra in *Agamemnon* for example.

All these devices were employed by Aeschylus, but what signals him out as the inventor of tragedy as we know it is his use of dialogue. Traditionally plays centred around the protagonist and the Chorus. Aeschylus added other characters who dialogued. And this gives us the stuff of drama as we know it.

Before we consider the moral issues that are at the core of the *Oresteia* it is important to outline the two plays following *Agamemnon*. The second play in the trilogy is *The Choephori*, sometimes known as *The Libation Bearers*. Seven years after the murder of Agamemnon his son Orestes returns from banishment to Phocis. He, with his friend Pylades, visits his father's grave – a mound of earth outside Athens for there had been no funeral rites for Agamemnon. He sees his sister Electra bringing wine as a libation for her father, which later transpires to be at the behest of her anxious mother, called by Electra "the mocker of gods, blasphemer of motherhood." Eventually the hidden Orestes reveals himself to Electra and there is a long section when Electra, Orestes and the Chorus try to awaken the spirit of Agamemnon to embolden their revenge on Clytemnestra. It is also told that Clytemnestra had a disturbing dream with a snake at her breast, drawing forth both milk and blood. Reasonably enough Orestes identifies with the snake. All lament "Oh, when will this suffering end?" It would seem that only Zeus can end the curse on the house of Atreus.

Orestes (and Pylades) in disguise arrive at the palace and inform Clytemnestra that Orestes is dead. She professes sorrow and grief?; though the real sorrow and grief are expressed by the Nurse who has been both the nurse and laundress of Orestes as a child. Unaware of the irony, Clytemnestra welcomes Orestes – "As our guest, call this your home" – and invites him to have a bath. Aegisthus goes to see the messenger who has brought news of Orestes' death and is stabbed and killed by Orestes. After a short debate with Pylades, in which Orestes acknowledges that "to kill a mother is terrible", Orestes lays aside any lasting doubts and knifes Clytemnestra, who dies silently, with a little dignity. The bodies of Clytemnestra and Aegisthus are revealed in the *ekkylema* wrapped in the bloody robe in which Agamemnon met his death. The Chorus is delighted and repeats: "This glorious day has set/The throne of Argos free" and are now confident that the throne of Argos having been purged "Our prince ... will ... rule the land with justice."

Of course it is not all finished. The vengeance of "like for like, for those who killed my father" may have been enacted. But now Orestes is a mother-killer and this as an activity cannot be sanctioned. Orestes comments that: "At this moment I am like a man/Driving a team of horses and not knowing where/The gallop's going to end." Just about the last words of the play are: "When shall be solved this long feud's argument?"

Which is where we turn to *The Eumenides, The Kindly Ones*, for there the solution lies, a solution in keeping with the then spirit of democracy in Athens. The play opens outside Apollo's temple at Delphi. Inside Orestes is promised by Apollo that as his "constant guardian" he "will not fail him." For the moment Apollo has put to sleep the Furies, described as "black, utterly loathsome" who dwell in subterranean Tartarus and who are the avengers of patricide and matricide. They have Orestes firmly in their sights. But while they are sleeping Orestes agrees to go to Athens and to put his case before Athene, the goddess of wisdom. Accompanied, to ensure his safety, by Hermes, Orestes reaches Athens. Meanwhile in Delphi the Furies have been awakened[3] by Clytemnestra's ghost demanding vengeance and they track Orestes to Athens by following the smell of his blood.

Orestes, seeking sanctuary before the temple of Athene, pleads to be washed clean of matricide. Athene herself appears, hears the case of the freshly arrived Chorus/Furies who assert that "We are the children of primeval night" who "drive out murderers." Although the Furies hear Athene's initial reaction that the Furies "seek the form of justice, more than to be just", they agree to trust Athene's wisdom and to give her the final decision on how to deal with Orestes. Orestes too says to Athene, "I will accept your word, for life or death." Having then heard Orestes' story Athene sees the case as "too grave a cause for any man to judge" and, partly because of her uncertainty about how to handle the Furies should they be deemed to have lost their case, Athene decides to select twelve "jurors of homicide" of Athens's wisest citizens "sworn to give sentence with integrity and truth."

The trial begins and Apollo speaks on behalf of Orestes: he argues that Zeus is the real source of all Apollo's pronouncements and views; that treachery was at the heart of the murder of

Agamemnon; unconvincingly he argues that there is a finality about murder; and finally argues that the father is the only true parent, whereas the mother is merely "a nurse who tends the growth of young seed."[4] He concludes by attempting to bribe Athene with the promise of many gifts. The Furies have history and logic on **their** side.

Before the jurors cast their votes, by black and white stones, Athene establishes this method of judgment as "a court inviolable … keeping faithful watch that men may sleep in peace." She also discloses that she will have the final say if the votes are equal and, in that case, she would "uphold Orestes' plea." Of course it is a complex and fraught situation. Not surprisingly the voting is six on either side. Which means that Orestes, by the casting vote of Athene, is acquitted of blood-guiltiness and the curse of the House of Atreus is finally lifted. Orestes departs to rule Argos, vowing that his country will always be a "staunch and faithful ally to the Athenian State."

The Eumenides, though is not over. Hanging over the whole trial has been the threat from the Furies that: "if we should fail to win this case/We will infest the land with plagues unspeakable." Fortunately – or skilfully – Athene succeeds in persuading the Furies that they will have a better life living under the earth in Athens with the role of protecting the city. All is resolved. The women of Athens can thank Zeus for the conclusion and it can be claimed that "When liberty and rule are balanced well/Success will follow as the gift of God." Not only this, for the principle of citizenship involvement in the state through juries, the democratic and educative process, the establishment of mercy as a valuable precedent – all these have been demonstrated and upheld by *The Eumenides*. All to the greater glory of the spirit of sixth century Athens.

Twice in the above narrative I have mentioned the House of Atreus and the curse hanging over it, the curse which was finally removed by the absolution of Orestes. I need to explain this. Agamemnon and Menelaus were sons of Atreus and it was their father's crimes that began the cycle of killing and revenge. Long before the action of the *Oresteian*, Atreus and his brother Thyestes murdered their half-brother Chrysippus to prevent him becoming king of Olympia and to make themselves next in line for that throne. For this crime their father banished them and they were given sanctuary in Mycenae. Recognizing their royal blood they were given temporary control of Argos while the king thereof, Eurystheus, went off into battle where he was killed. So Atreus and Thyestes became permanent kings at Mycenae.

Permanent is the wrong word, for almost immediately there was dissension between the brothers. Initially Thyestes took the throne and then Atreus; Atreus banished Thyestes. Artemis, Hermes and Zeus (and a golden lamb) were all involved in the in-fighting between the brothers. When Atreus then discovered that Thyestes had had an affair with his – Atreus' – wife Aerope, he planned the most appalling revenge. He killed the sons of Thyestes and cooked them and served them up as a feast for their unwitting father. According to Seneca in his play *Thyestes* the sons of Atreus, Agamemnon and Menelaus, were complicit in the plot.

The skullduggery and moral abomination does not end there, though. Far from it. Desperately desirous for revenge, Thyestes heeds the words of an oracle who promises him that if he had a son by his daughter Pelopia, that son would kill Atreus. Disguised he rapes his daughter and she bears a son – Aegisthus! In time Aegisthus kills Atreus. Thyestes rules Mycenae! Until, with the help of King Tyndareus of Sparta, to where they had been exiled, Agamemnon and Menelaus reclaim the throne from Thyestes. We hear no more of Thyestes.

That, then, is the background to *The Oresteian Trilogy*: a sequence of crimes against nature with an involvement of various gods. In Seneca's *Thyestes* the last words of Thyestes to his brother are: "The gods will take revenge, I leave you to their care for punishment." Fortunately Athene, in her wisdom, can see beyond punishment and thereby permits Aeschylus to show the curse on the house of Atreus being worked out and brought to an end: what initially appeared to be intractable issues have been resolved.

Before we spell out more clearly these issues, a few words about characterisation. When we come to consider tragedians like Shakespeare and Ibsen the delineation of character is central to the drama – not so with the classical Greek playwrights. But although the Chorus has a chameleon nature – in the trilogy they represent successively twelve Elders of Argos, Clytemnestra's female servants and the Furies – the main protagonists do possess some identifiable characteristics. In all three plays Clytemnestra is presented as a strong woman; Agamemnon's arrogance is established in his first speech; Aegisthus is branded a coward and a lecher by the Elders/Chorus, but he is not bombastic and is (apparently) reasoned and calm in his explanations of his involvement with the plot. Of course he is killed towards the end of *Agamemnon*, but in a different universe I would have liked to have experienced more of the character of Aegisthus. It is Orestes, though, who is the central character in *The Oresteian Trilogy*: I have already quoted his words about his driving a team of galloping horses, with a weakened grip, and not knowing where his journey will end. That uncertainty, hence anxiety, is echoed all through the presentation of Orestes.

Characterisation, though, is neither the forte nor the main concern of Aeschylus. His poetry – like that of Sophocles and, perhaps especially, Euripides and Seneca – is at times splendid[5], but it is the philosophical issues that are Aeschylus's main concern.

When reading – or, hopefully – seeing, *The Oresteian Trilogy* one of the underlying themes we need to be aware of is that of the replacement of the old gods by the new ones. The Furies, dwelling beneath the earth, were representatives of the old chthonian gods (*chthon* means earth), representing fear and death, whereas the new Olympian religion, with Zeus at the forefront, was associated with joy and celebration. Defending Orestes, Apollo claims to be the spokesman for Zeus and the final verdict is a victory for the new gods over the old ones, and is totally in tune with the democratic and celebratory mood of sixth-century Athens.

It is the Furies who equate justice with vengeance and demand retribution, but I think it important not to gainsay the human responses to the murder of a loved one. Forgiveness for such a deed is rare: even today it is natural to demand blood for blood – instinctive human reaction has not changed. So although on one level the gods are clearly involved in *The Oresteian Trilogy*, there is a human level which is very real. Your daughter has been killed by your husband – you want revenge. Your father has been murdered by your mother and her lover – you want revenge. And then you are burdened with matricide – can this ever be condoned? On a human level this is what *The Oresteian Trilogy* is all about. Similar human dilemmas have to be confronted by Hamlet and Prospero too.

There is the issue too of Fate and freedom. The House of Atreus was cursed long before *Agamemnon* began: Agamemnon, Aegisthus and Orestes are all victims of that curse. Do they have choices, do they have free will? Perhaps this is where we distinguish Destiny from Fate. You inherit a destiny but you do not have to accept that you are in the hands of a fate that allows you no choices. The Chorus of Elders of Argos points this out at the beginning of *Agamemnon*: Fate gives you a choice and Agamemnon, in sacrificing Iphigenia, chose wrongly. That was a sin, after which:

> "…he put on **of his own will** [my highlighting]
> The harness of Necessity."

This whole issue of fate, freedom, destiny, free will, predestination, being programmed and so on is still one to keep undergraduates discussing through the wee small hours of the morning. *The Oresteian Trilogy* can contribute meaningfully to such a discussion.

In the introduction to this series of essays I commented upon the importance of suffering for the tragic hero and the wisdom gained thereby. We will see this more powerfully when we consider Sophocles's Oedipus, but there is no doubt that Orestes emerges from his suffering experiences wiser, more settled and more able to govern Argos. It could be argued, though, that the main learning from *The Oresteian Trilogy* is for the citizens of Athens. They have witnessed an enactment of the trials of the House of Atreus, wrestling with the eternal question of how to do right and how to have justice. "What is justice?" has been the question all through the trilogy. And by the end of *The Eumenides* they have an answer.

As I was recounting the story, and backstory, of *The Oresteian Trilogy*, the issues I have just discussed were both implicit and explicit in the telling – but not the answer. Not until we arrive at the closing scenes of *The Eumenides*. There we have reconciliation with the old powers/the powers of darkness: a role has been found for the Furies – they have been accommodated into civilized society. (Doubtless to Freud's delight.) And there has been an acknowledgment that many decisions are difficult but democracy, with the voice of the informed individual, and the jury system are best placed to provide answers. The final outcome is thus a restoration of order, celebrated by the citizens of Athens with a joyous torchlit procession, with music and singing. We have come a long way from the plains of Argos, with Clytemnestra eagerly waiting to kill her husband and so perpetuating the curse on the House of Atreus. Reason has triumphed over revenge.

---

[1] Homer's stories were very well known in Greece.

[2] She actually says that Orestes was "our only hope to charm the curse of the house from running triumphantly amuck."

[3] So revolting was the first appearance of the haggard Furies that it was reported that one female spectator had a heart attack and died on the spot.

[4] A dreadful argument! The woman acting as a "mere" vessel to carry the man's seed! I cannot imagine even the most rabid misogynist agreeing with this. Feminists too (indeed most of us) are also likely to be horrified that Athena's judgement is based on "the father's claim and male supremacy in all things" – though she does reserve for herself the right of choice when she "give(s) herself in marriage."

[5] My knowledge of Greek (and Latin) is limited, so I have chosen not to quote examples of the poetry, as these examples would be in translation and therefore it would be the translator's words that I would be praising.

SOPHOCLES: *The Theban Plays*

There can be little doubt that Sophocles was the greatest of the Athenian playwrights. Not only did Aristotle use *King Oedipus*[1] as an exemplar of the tragic form at its best, but Sophocles won, by most calculations, some twenty-four of the thirty competitions in which he entered and was never adjudged any lower than second place. Two thirds of these victories were in the major spring Dionysian festivals and the others in the Lenaea festivals in late January. In a league table of competition winners Sophocles comes first with 24 wins, Aeschylus second with 14 and Euripides way behind with a mere 4.

Sophocles was born in 496 BC, some twenty-nine years after Aeschylus. Sophocles did beat Aeschylus in competition (notably in 468 BC), but most of his successes and fame were subsequent to the death of Aeschylus. Although, as we shall see, Sophocles questions many establishment values in his plays he was very much part of the Athenian wealthy class. In fact, unlike Aeschylus, Sophocles never left Athens, though his fame as a playwright meant that he received many invitations to do so. His father was a manufacturer of armour and he himself, besides being a close friend of the eminent statesman Pericles, served at different times as a city treasurer and as a naval officer. He was actively involved in the splendour of Athenian democracy – though, as he lived to the age of ninety, he also experienced the defeat of Athens by other city states in the Peloponnesian War.

There are some, I would think far-fetched, rumours about how Sophocles died, but one story about his latter years is worth repeating. Apparently his sons – presumably for reasons of having some control of his finances – took him to court to have him declared incompetent. Sophocles effectively refuted this charge by reading from *Oedipus at Colonus* which had not yet been produced.

In fact *Oedipus at Colonus* was first staged by Sophocles' grandson some four years after his death. So although chronologically vis-à-vis the unfolding of events in the Theban plays it is placed second, it was in fact the last to be written. Whereas *Antigone*, which concludes the sequence of three plays we have was the first to be written. Although this makes for some inconsistencies between the plays I think it makes sense to publish them or act them in the traditional sequence of *King Oedipus, Oedipus at Colonus, Antigone*. All these plays were taken from different tetralogies. I suppose we are fortunate that these three plays survived, together with four other plays[2], but we are desperately unfortunate that another one hundred and sixteen referenced plays of Sophocles are lost.

Stylistically there are two ways in which Sophocles advanced Greek theatre. Firstly there is what Aristotle called skenographia, or scenery-painting: we have an example of this in *Oedipus at Colonus* where the Chorus graphically describes the battle between the forces of Theseus and Creon for the recapture of Antigone and Ismene and, perhaps more purely, there is the Chorus's lengthy, evocative description of Colonus – "Of all earth's lovely lands the loveliest." Secondly, though, and most importantly the innovation to which we are most indebted to Sophocles is the addition of a third character in the dialogue (which Aeschylus copied in his later plays): the Chorus, although still always relevant as a commentator and sounding-board, assumes a less dominant role and inter-personal dialogue develops. And not only inter-personal dialogue, but real characterisation develops. Consciously Sophocles allowed characters to be more than one dimensional and to express their personal feelings. There is a wonderful example of this when, in *Antigone*, the Sentry makes two appearances, in the first one having to confess to Creon that someone unbeknown to the three sentries has buried the body of Philoctetes, and in the second one bringing the captured Antigone to Creon. Not only does the Sentry conduct an almost stream of consciousness dialogue with himself, he fears and reasons with and stands up to Creon. There is something of the Porter in *Macbeth* and the Gravedigger in *Hamlet* about him, but basically he is the complex creation of Sophocles. With the conscious individualisation of character, theatre is becoming drama.

There are issues to be discussed in *The Theban Plays* which to a greater or lesser extent are to be found in most complex drama, but before they are looked at I want to give a brief outline of the story of the plays. That puts the reader in the position of the Greek audience of the time: the stories – as in fact with nearly all of Shakespeare's[3] plays – were well-known: it is what the dramatist does with the stories that matters.

The chronological story is as follows. Oedipus as a baby was riveted by his ankles in a wooded hollow of Cithaeron, having been rejected by his parents Laius and Jocasta and left to die there. He was rejected in order that the prophecy that he would kill his father and marry his mother would not be fulfilled. A shepherd rescued him from the mountainside and Oedipus eventually became the adopted son of King Polybus and Queen Merope of Corinth. Once he heard of the patricide prophecy, not knowing that he had been adopted as an infant, Oedipus left Corinth and went travelling. At a place where three roads meet he was accosted by Laius and in the ensuing fight Oedipus unwittingly killed his father. Oedipus moves on to Thebes where he solves the riddle of the sphinx that had been devastating Thebes and is given, as a reward, the hand of Jocasta in marriage – it having been reported that Laius had been killed by robbers. In fact Oedipus with his mother/wife rule for fifteen years and have four children together (two sons and two daughters), before the horrific truth slowly emerges. Jocasta hangs herself, Oedipus blinds himself. Eventually he leaves Thebes and his brother-in-law Creon is left to rule.

That is the story of *King Oedipus*. In *Oedipus at Colonus* we find Oedipus in a rustic landscape in the hamlet of Colonus, only a mile away from Athens. Creon had permitted the blinded Oedipus to live on in Athens but years later exiles him. So he is now "white-haired, blind and in squalid garments", accompanied by his younger daughter Antigone. His elder daughter Ismene has frequently found ways of reporting what has been going on in Thebes but now she comes in person to tell news of fighting between her two brothers over the rulership of Thebes. Polynices has enlisted the support of the armies of Argos and is battling against his younger brother Eteocles who expelled him from Thebes. Theseus, King of Athens, promises protection for Oedipus (and Antigone). Creon then arrives from Thebes, imploring Oedipus to return home, believing that maybe that will lift the curse and warfare that is besetting Athens. "My everlasting curse upon your country!" is the reply of

Oedipus. Whereupon Creon abducts Antigone and Ismene, and Theseus keeps his promise and, through the battle I previously mentioned vis-à-vis a description of it given by the Chorus, he is victorious and returns the two daughters to their father. Polynices then appears and asks his father –"both you and I are homeless exiles" – to help him retake Thebes from his brother. Oedipus refuses and Polynices, taking a last leave from his already mourning sister Antigone, leads his Argos army against Thebes to certain defeat. Finally "as one inspired with inward vision" Oedipus, accompanied by Theseus, walks off almost into the sunset, leaving Theseus to assist in the safe return of Antigone and Ismene to Thebes.

Antigone is the shortest of the three plays. Before the play opens there has been a battle for rulership of Thebes between the brothers Eteocles and Polynices, in the course of which each brother killed the other in personal combat, leaving Creon once more to rule Thebes, a Thebes that has successfully withstood the assault from the Polynices-led army from Argos. Eteocles, as a defender of Thebes, is given an honourable ritual burial, while Creon decrees that Polynices should be left without ceremony and unburied outside the city wall for beasts to devour. Antigone will not accept this treatment of her brother and twice defies Creon's edict. The second time she is seen and arrested by the sentries, brought before Creon and sentenced to death for defying the law. (Ismene too, by association, and not by action, is too sentenced to death.) Haemon, the only surviving son of Creon and Eurydice, had been betrothed to Antigone; initially seeming to accept his father's verdict on Antigone he eventually convinces him to free her. But this is all too late for Antigone; she commits suicide, as then do both Haemon and Eurydice, leaving Creon with an overwhelming burden of guilt and the Chorus to have the final words: "We learn when we are old." The curse on the house of Labdacus[4] is over.

In these synopses of the three plays I have deliberately foregone any mention of the part played by the gods, though in reality there is scarcely a page when their responsibility/culpability is not at the forefront. The central issues of Fate and Freedom and of God's law and Human law I will discuss later, but I want to try to get a handle on the gods of classical mythology/drama to help render them comprehensible to today's audiences. Manifestly they are external forces beyond our control unless our entreaties – imploring, placating, encouraging, usually by prayer, worship or offerings – can resonate with them and bring about a change in attitude or behaviour. That, I suppose, is not unlike a Christian asking for divine intervention from his God. But we have no equivalent of the range of Greek/Roman gods in the twenty-first century.

So, granted that the tensions between the gods and mortals produces first rate drama, is there any way that we today can accept the concept of the classical gods? On an everyday level we can see the gods as an externalisation of our internal impulses – to love, fight, retreat, console etc. – impulses that, at different times, we need either to control or encourage. The Greeks asked the gods to assist them: we look inwards, through the focus given by meditation and prayer, and seek a measure of personal control over these impulses.

I think that is true enough, but that way of thinking does not do justice to the superhuman power of the classical gods. Maybe it is better to see them in association with Carl Jung's collective unconscious where chthonic, atavistic energies roam. According to Jung we each inherit the common collective unconscious: it is a psychic system of a collective, universal and impersonal nature which is identical in all individuals.[5] Although Jung personifies it as a Wise Old Man, atavistic forces can suddenly spring up from – apparently – nowhere and the individual can find her/himself behaving in a way totally out of ego-controlled character. This eruption of feeling, which is scarcely controllable however we attempt to combat it, can make us feel helpless, at the mercy of forces beyond our command, so that we are no longer in control of what we thought was a reasonably ordered life. Our fate is no longer exclusively in our own hands. And **that** was also the effect of the gods on classical society. These gods hidden deep in our psyche can, viewed positively, give us numinous/spiritual insights, or, according to Jung, represent hell.

The collective unconscious theory does, I hope, do justice to the power of the gods and the ultimate helplessness experienced by the protagonists in classical tragedy. It is a way of trying to reconcile the realities of the classical gods with the realities of what can be climate change realities of twenty-first century life. On stage an intelligent audience, involved in the drama before it, probably has no problem in accepting the realness of the gods, but maybe in the cold light of day, when the rational mind takes over, an explanation of the concept of the gods is needed. That is what I have attempted to give.

But what are the major issues dramatised by Sophocles? Personal freedom, as distinct from being a pawn in the hands of the gods, is undoubtedly a central theme. Early in *King Oedipus* Jocasta resignedly proclaims:

"Chance rules our lives, and the future is all unknown.
Best live as best we may, from day to day"

and similarly the Chorus in *Oedipus at Colonus* comments:

"No man has ever lived out of the reach
Of misadventure's grasping hand."

It is true that the Theban plays contain many fewer references to the need to negotiate with gods than do Aeschylus' *Oresteian Trilogy* but the gods are a present force and the oracle of Apollo at Delphi is especially significant. That is where the initial presaging of the disaster of the son killing his father and marrying his mother began, which not only is the instigator of the series of events that beset the house of Labdacus but which also poses the question of whether Oedipus has control, over his fate: is he freely fated or fatefully free, as George Schrader has it?

Oedipus sees himself as "the child of fortune" and Theseus labels him "the world's most ill-used man." One's first thought is to share Oedipus' view and to feel for him in his unwanted, apparently inescapable, plight. Yet character too is part of destiny, and Sophocles, character-delineating, draws our attention to the hubris of Oedipus. It is as though he accepts the comments of the Chorus that he is both the first and greatest of men. Having initially welcomed Teiresias the blind soothsayer as there being nothing beyond his ken, he turns on him when Teiresias insists that the killer of Laius is present and boasts that it was he, Oedipus, who solved the riddle of the sphinx by his mother-wit, something which the bird-lore of Teiresias could not do. The Chorus comments that "Pride kills the tyrant" and Oedipus boasts that "I have saved this land from ruin. I am content." In addition he could claim that he and Jocasta ruled successfully for fifteen years.

There is further example of the hubris of Oedipus in *Oedipus at Colonus*: his daughter Ismene comes from Thebes with the news that "the present oracles" are saying that the return of Oedipus to Thebes will bring a much needed peace to that city. Later in the play, when both Creon and, separately, his son Polynices make a similar plea, the latter promising that "I shall restore you to your rightful place", the response from Oedipus to the request to return is an angry dismissal of them, together with a death curse on Polynices and his brother Eteocles. I am not sure that he has learned the necessary lesson of humility: self is put before country. He seems both to believe and to contradict his own words: "I am a holy man, and by holy ordinance/My presence here is to bring this people blessing." The point is that, irrespective of the curse on the house of Labdacus, the proud and easy to anger Oedipus is riding for a fall.

This matter of our freedom to act and a fate that descends on us and takes away our control of our lives is of fundamental concern for all mankind. In many religions – in the doctrine of predestination in Christianity for example – there is a quiescent acceptance of one's life being in the hands of God/Allah. That certainly is the mood of the Theban plays. Ultimately I think it is an imponderable question. It is probably true that we never know when fate or bad luck may deal us an unexpected blow that throws our lives completely off course and it is pointless being so self-protective and shoring up one's life against all possible fateful interventions that one ceases to live. (Though I might add that if you build your life, either in reality or metaphorically upon a flood plane, you are courting disaster.) For me I would accept the words of Jocasta "Best live as best we may, from day to day", but I would add **"as though** we are free."

Law and justice is another theme explored by Sophocles. And it is complicated by the belief that the gods also have their laws that we humans should respond to – which is basically no different from the sometime conflict between the laws and commandments of a religion and the laws of the state. Theseus in *Oedipus at Colonus* is adamant: "Our is a land/That lives by justice, knows no rule but law" and although Creon, when first lecturing on the importance of obeying the law as decreed by the state's appointee, says he will never disobey it, things change: Antigone makes a strong case for the laws of the gods licensing her burial of her brother –"what law of heaven have I transgressed/" and Haemon too reinforces her argument, stripping it down to the basics of being a question of "right and wrong." And Creon has to acknowledge finally that "It is by the laws of heaven that man must live." So it is no good Oedipus, again showing his pride and lack of humility, claiming: "The law/Acquits me, innocent, as ignorant,/Of what I did." There is a law higher than any state's law which demands prior obedience.

The Theban plays pass comment on other issues that don't go away, but before I mention them I would like to draw attention to the beauty of the verse – again it is in translation but I think a taster is warranted. I have already alluded to the description of Colonus, but here is a sample from *Antigone*. Here is Haemon persuading his father to change his mind:

> "It is no weakness for the wisest man
> To learn when he is wrong, know when to yield.
> So, on the margin of a flooded river,
> Trees bending to the torrent live unbroken,
> While those that strain against it are snapped off.
> A sailor has to tack and slacken sheets
> Before the gale, or find himself capsized."

Beautifully expressed – and sound advice for anyone hiding behind self-righteous dogma.

I have mentioned the very real individualisation of the Sentry in *Antigone*. In the same play there is a subtlety about the arguments presented by and the characterisation of Haemon. Polynices too in *Oedipus at Colonus* is seen by his father as a scoundrel and cursed, whereas he does show loyalty to the troops from Argos he is leading and his sisters are completely acceptant of him. His is a fairly small part, but it is far from one dimensional. This is Sophocles beginning to create modern theatre.

Of course it is the gods' laws of family which Antigone, in her support for her brother, is also upholding. She expects too that her father and mother and Polynices would be in heaven to welcome her. Family issues are manifestly at the centre of the Oedipus story!

Theseus understands the importance of family: Oedipus' greeting of Antigone and Ismene, before he acknowledges their rescuer Theseus, is seen as right and understandable by Theseus. Indeed it is Theseus who emerges from the Theban plays as the good ruler and the kindest man. Oedipus' family loyalties extend only to his daughters and not to his sons, and Creon – in many ways the darkness to the light of Theseus – is in his arrogance ("I am a king, and responsible only to myself") responsible for the deaths of his son and daughter. Family has always mattered – the concept was not coined by *East Enders*!

When it comes to matters of gender there are indications that Sophocles' mindset was that of the day. Oedipus is scornful of his sons:

> "They ape Egyptian manners, do they,
> Where men keep house and do embroidery
> While wives go out to earn the daily bread?"

and Ismene implores her sister:

> "O think, Antigone; we are women; it is not for us
> To fight against men."

However, when we think of Antigone, and certainly if we compare her with Electra in Aeschylus' *Oresteian Trilogy*, we have a portrait, again individualised, of a real spunky lady. Attendant on her helpless father, standing up to Creon, Antigone refuses to be acceptably passive: "When I have **tried** and failed, I shall have failed" is her response to Ismene's caution. It is no wonder she refuses to let Ismene share her glory in death as Ismene chose to stay at home and not lend her support for the burial of Polynices. In passing, it is worth noting that the wisest person in the plays is Tiresias who is bi-gendered.

Those are the main issues emanating from the Theban plays. Self-will too gets a bad press. I am going to conclude this discussion of the writing of the greatest Greek playwright with quotations which, I hope, will give further insight into the mood of the plays. Firstly there is the power of the gods: "Aphrodite immortal works her will in all" ruefully comments the Chorus. Secondly there is the question of obedience to the law: "What law have heaven have I transgressed?" challenges Antigone. And finally, two quotations from *King Oedipus* which encapsulate the feelings and mood of the Chorus as, bystanders as we are, they witness the horror and tragedy of the house of Labdacus:

> "Show me the man whose happiness was anything more than illusion
> Followed by disillusion.
> Here is the instance, here is Oedipus, here is the reason
> Why I will call no mortal creature happy"

and –

> "Then learn that mortal man must always look to his ending,
> And no man can be called happy until the day when he carries
> His happiness down to the grave in peace."

---

[1] Also known as *King Oedipus* or *Oedipus Rex*.

[2] *Ajax*, *The Women of Trachis*, *Electra* and *Philoctetes*.

[3] The only plays of Shakespeare for which a source cannot be found are *Love's Labour's Lost* and *The Tempest*.

[4] Labdacus was a grandson of Cadmus, the founder of Thebes, and the father of Laius.

[5] We also possess our own individual unconscious.

PHAEDRA

Euripides: **Hippolytus**
Seneca: **Phaedra**
Racine: **Phèdre**

A person of some stature, humbled and suffering, an identifiable representative of humankind who, through suffering, gains insight into what life is all about – that is the essence of tragedy. So far we have witnessed resolutions to the curses visited on the houses of Atreus and Labdacus respectively – order has been restored and this in itself is a valid comment on the major priority of state and society. But have the protagonists, Orestes and Oedipus, gained the consciousness and wisdom that Aristotle hoped for? Orestes learned something about loyalty to family and family loyalty was again in evidence in the Theban Plays, but shown by Antigone, rather than Oedipus. The main learning, though, in these two sequences of plays was about the inescapability of fate, the inevitable misery in being human and the power of the gods over individual human life. With the result that Oedipus, in particular, humbled and brought down to earth as he was, could, to the end, rail against the gods and deny any personal responsibility for his fate. I do not think that is sufficient personal insight.

When we consider the Phaedra myth, however, we see, in all three writers[1], a depiction of acceptance of personal responsibility. Phaedra anguishes before (and indeed after) she acts. Sophocles began to give us real characterisation but ostensibly in the minor parts; Euripides powerfully individualised the main character, Phaedra, and both Seneca and Racine continue to explore the internal dilemma of Phaedra.

The basic myth/story of Phaedra and Hippolytus is the same in all three dramas. Phaedra is married to Theseus who has a son, Hippolytus, by a previous marriage to the Amazon queen Hippolyta. Hippolytus is a huntsman and scorns (the company of) women. Although she fights against it, Phaedra lusts after her stepson. Both Hippolytus and Theseus get to know this: Hippolytus is horrified and Theseus, believing his son to be the wrong-wisher, invokes the sea-god Neptune to punish Hippolytus by death. Driving his chariot away from Athens, Hippolytus meets a hideous death by the seashore. Phaedra admits her guilt and commits suicide and Theseus is mortified. All three writers would not demur from that description, but, as ever, it is how they deal with the story that matters. I now want to look at all three of the plays: on one hand to show the development of self-awareness and internal dialogue in the plays and, on the other, to show how they all contribute to this central issue of freedom, responsibility and fate – central not only to the whole topic of tragedy but also central to everyone's approach to life.

At first sight Euripides' *Hippolytus* seems not dissimilar to the already discussed plays by Aeschylus and Sophocles. The goddess Aphrodite opens the play, saying how the gods enjoy receiving honour from the human race and how Hippolytus calls her "the most pernicious of the heavenly powers." And how, as a consequence of this insult, "(he) shall suffer for it." Soon after the huntsmen accompanying Hippolytus hail the hunter-goddess Artemis as "the loveliest of immortal maids" and Hippolytus says of Aphrodite "to me she is nothing at all." Looking at things from Aphrodite's perspective, Hippolytus is asking for it, and, therefore, of course gets it. At the end of *Hippolytus* Theseus laments "I was cheated by the gods out of my right mind", and Artemis tries to console Theseus with the words: "men may well sin, when the gods so ordain." So, yes, from that perspective, the gods control the fate of man.

There is too the family history which has to be played out. Phaedra is the sister of Ariadne who helped Theseus find the minotaur in the Cretan labyrinth and kill it. Theseus and Ariadne then ran off together, but Theseus tired of her and left her on Naxos where Dionysus claimed her as his bride. But there is more. Phaedra and Ariadne were the daughters of King Minos and Pasiphae. Minos had the labyrinth designed and constructed by Daedalus in order to contain the minotaur[2], but Pasiphae also employed Daedalus – to construct a wooden cow for her to go inside so that she could be ravaged by the minotaur. As Theseus laments:

"O Fate, like a cruel heel crushing me and my house...
Long ago a sin was sown."

And Phaedra acknowledges her mother's lust for a bull and how her sister suffered for love – "the curse that destroyed them I now inherit." Theseus and Phaedra suffer as a result of their family's past history: a familiar theme.

Does Hippolytus, however, deserve to suffer and die, and die so violently too? I find him, as Euripides undoubtedly meant me to, incredibly arrogant. His disdain for Aphrodite and his self-righteous denial of any sex drive (which Racine plays with) probably deserve a come-uppance. Notice also that as he dies in his father's arms he boasts that "you will never meet a man more honourable" and his final words are "I here absolve you of my death ...Pray that your true-born sons may be like me!" What an arrogant prick!

In contrast to the virtuous Hippolytus we have the would-be incestuous mother-in-law. Yet all our sympathies are for Phaedra. Hippolytus at one moment rails against women: "O Zeus! Why have you plagued this world with so vile and worthless a thing as a woman? Better that men... should buy themselves children... Curse the whole race of you! I can never hate you enough!" The Chorus too has no high regard for women: "...women are always weak, and their ways are strange/Their very being is a blend of terror and helplessness." Yet in his presentation of Phaedra Euripides gives the complete lie to these ready judgments. We witness a woman struggling against the uncontrollable hot blood of her lust for Hippolytus. She knows it to be wrong and she is trying to "find a way to bring honour out of shame." And when her nurse betrays her feelings to Hippolytus and so shows her secret to the world, Phaedra realises that, wrong as she was, the nurse acted out of love "to cure my suffering." If we don't have the internal debate of the soliloquy, as Shakespeare gives us, we have an ongoing dialogue with the nurse as to how to resolve the human dilemma of lusting after the forbidden. This wrestling with what it is to be human and attempting to control unbidden drives is the stuff of drama – and indeed life.

There are two more aspects of Euripides' *Hippolytus* to which I want to draw attention. As ever we find words of wisdom in Greek plays. Even Hippolytus has his moment of truth: "For a wise man a throne has no attraction; to find pleasure in power is to be corrupted by it – there are many examples." I rather like the Nurse's comment too: "After all, wisdom is only happening to guess right."

It's a Greek play, so there are so many references to fate – fate being "purposeless and blind"; disaster following disaster; there being no escape; no rest from travail and toil; certainly no happiness! But Euripides' understanding of humanity shines through. I think this final quotation underlines that truth. It is said by the Nurse: "In human life second thoughts often prove to be wiser. What has happened to you is nothing extraordinary or hard to understand …When love sweeps on in the fullness of her power, there is no resisting …how many good and sensible husbands see their wives unfaithful and look the other way?… Why, the true wisdom for mortals is to keep faults well hidden …it's not for us mortals to struggle after a tiresome perfection …You are mortal, child …You are in love: then bear – and dare – what the god has willed."

When we turn to Seneca's *Phaedra*, written some four hundred and fifty years after Euripides's play, the first thing we notice is the absence of the power of the gods. True there are references made to various gods. But in no way is this presented as a duel between Aphrodite and Artemis. The inexorable nature of fate is played down too, but it is there in the references made to the family from which Phaedra comes: right at the beginning of the play Phaedra laments "the women of Crete can never enjoy an easy love. They always have monstrous affairs"; and Theseus too recognises the power of heredity – "if only we could escape/the link of nature chaining parents to their blood!" he cries and apropos of Hippolytus he comments:

> "Our family is regressing,
> Tainted blood reverts to its ancestry.
> That madness is typical of the warrior race:
> first despising sex, then whoring out
> That long-preserved virginity."

So fate is presented in terms of inherited family genes. The portrait of the individual protagonists is so much more detailed, particularly in the case of Theseus. In Euripides's *Hippolytus* Theseus is shown as spending a year in exile in Troezen to atone for the blood he has shed, whereas Seneca has Phaedra complaining that he is showing her his usual faithfulness in having gone off on a quest for "rape and forbidden sex."

Arguably this gives a plausible reason for Phaedra's anger at her husband and, seeing the young Theseus in Hippolytus, she lusts after him, almost uncontrollably. The real point, though, about Phaedra's passion is that it is **not** reasonable; it comes from within and overwhelms her. We hear from her nurse that, typical of so many lovers in literature, she forgets to sleep, has no interest in food or health, is riddled with anxiety and even "trembles as she walks." As in Euripides' play Phaedra is ashamed of her desires, but in Seneca's play it is she who directly confronts Hippolytus and confesses her love for him, and the two plays diverge thence both in their narrative and in Phaedra's response. Here Hippolytus draws his sword on Phaedra and the Nurse, and when the Nurse suggests that they "flip the crime around" and cries "rape", Hippolytus runs away, dropping his sword in his haste. Phaedra goes along with the Nurse's suggestion and tells Theseus that although her heart did not yield her "body put up with the violence." Theseus believes her and invokes Neptune to fashion the usual death of Hippolytus by the seashore, via a tsunami and a bull from the sea and the subsequent panic of his horses, throwing his body to the ground and shattering his skull.

With Seneca there is no final reconciliation between father and son. Phaedra, however, regrets her lies, confesses the reality to Theseus, the reality of Hippolytus' chasteness and purity, kills herself and, as the Chorus says, Theseus is left with "infinite time for tears." Hippolytus will then be given full funeral rites and Theseus prepares himself for chaos, hell and death. But there is no forgiveness for Phaedra.

So Phaedra does not rely on the Nurse's deceit in Seneca's play: there is less lovesick angst and more strong personal confrontation than with Euripides. Her plight and its resolution, though, remain identical. The ultimate fate of Hippolytus is, of course, the same in all three plays too, but Seneca fine-tunes him and, in doing so, makes him for me the most interesting character in the play.

Yes, he is obnoxious. He boasts of wandering in innocence through the countryside, being innocent and devoid of anger, lust and greed. The Nurse reminds him that he is young and that therefore he should "go out to late-night parties." Young people should be happy and should not gloomily despise sex. Yet Hippolytus is adamant that his life is both right and righteous. In common with Euripides, Seneca gives Hippolytus similar thoughts about stepmothers[3] too: that "beasts are more kind." He concludes that "Woman is the root of all evil."

Yet, although there is a good deal of prim moralising in his long speech in response to the Nurse in Act 2, there is actually also a good deal of awareness of the putrid values of the world – any world. He comments critically on the military and territorial acquisition; he dismisses "the futile goals of fame or fleeting wealth"; he is critical of the establishment and how the "wicked lust for money" and see the weak go to the wall where Might triumphed over Right. I am writing this two days after the death of Tony Benn who would, I think, have concurred with Hippolytus' political analysis. And, although he asserts of his stepmother that "no woman in the world can match your wickedness" he has a degree of self-awareness and self-criticism when he shouts: "I am evil, I deserve to die: I was attractive to my stepmother." So he is not simply a monodimensional sex/women hater. Perhaps he is too young to have apparently made up his mind on so many subjects, but his perspective on life is not uninteresting. When we come to Racine's Hippolytus we see an extension both of his dilemma and of his responses to life.

Manifestly, though, it is Phaedra's dilemma that is at the heart of all three plays – and it is the would-be incestuous stepmother who elicits our sympathies. Whether we see her as a playground for the conflicting demands of Artemis and Aphrodite, thus externalising her internal conflict, or whether we acknowledge that she is struggling to control her passion with her reason, her dilemma is a common one: how do we respond to an overwhelming inappropriate urge? Can we control a visceral response? Whether we label the unwanted drive love or lust – and there is certainly a discussion to be had about this, which could use a starting point the early comment of the Nurse in Seneca's play "The fiction that love is a god was created by base lust/yielding to degradation" – there is no doubt that this split of conflicting demands is something most of us experience at least once in a lifetime. There are primitive, atavistic forces lying low in the collective unconscious common to all which occasionally – like the Cretan minotaur demanding to be fed – thrust themselves upwards to our personal consciousness and can for a time, take over our being and behaviour. With Phaedra it is lust which surfaces.

This conflict is expressed in Racine's *Phèdre* when Phèdre talks of "my madness ... I have crossed all bounds of decency" and when Phèdre doubts that she could govern any state "when my reason cannot govern me." This latter comment is made believing Theseus to be dead, leaving Athens needing a new ruler. Clearly this adds a new dimension, for whereas with Seneca, we expect the return of Theseus, as he is away assisting his friend Pirithous steal the wife of Hades, Persephone, from the underworld, here he initially has gone missing and then, mistakenly, is reported dead. As Oenone, Phèdre's nurse, points out Theseus' death makes loving Hippolytus no longer an illegal act. Which makes it easier for Phèdre to approach Hippolytus directly and confess her passion for him. (Previously Phèdre had successfully sought the banishment of Hippolytus to Trozene, claiming that she was a new wife and jealous of the closeness of Theseus and Hippolytus – but really trying to get rid of the lust she was experiencing for Hippolytus. But then Theseus had brought Phèdre to Trozene too.)

When Phèdre tells Hippolytus of her desire for him he is, as in the other two plays, taken aback and horrified, but his response is not a priggish, self-righteous one – he just runs away from the situation. Similarly early in the play when his tutor Theramenes suggests that loving a woman is "something sweet to be tried" and asks him where he would be had his mother practised such "timid scruples" as Hippolytus does, this is a reply not to a self-righteous rant about the glories of the open air and chastity, but a reply to a much more thoughtful comment about his father's past behaviour with women – his deceit and aggression. Hippolytus does not want to be like that. There is, though, another reason why Hippolytus is so much less outspoken than he is in the other two plays. ("I never break a vow" is the strongest statement he makes.) And that is Aricia, an Athenian princess whose family had failed in its attempt to overthrow Theseus and which is now condemned to servitude. Theramenes has noticed Hippolytus' affection for Aricia, an affection not denied by Hippolytus but to which his response is to run away from Trozene on the pretext of looking for his missing father. Clearly pitched a few decibels lower than Phèdre's lust, Hippolytus is nonetheless fighting his feelings against his principles, as is Phèdre. It is a similar dilemma and adds an extra dimension to the plot. What happens is that Hippolytus releases Aricia from her servitude and promises her Athens to rule – there is no doubt of their mutual attraction, something they both lovingly acknowledge. Then Theseus returns and the Hippolytus/Phèdre wrangle assumes centre stage. Hippolytus dies by the seaside as we have become accustomed (another graphic and lengthy narrative) and Theseus' concluding words in *Phèdre* are:

"(We) shall take Aricia for our daughter. We
Shall pardon her her family's treachery."

Aricia thus makes Hippolytus much more human – an extra dimension is added to the exploration of the Phèdre myth.

Aricia also adds another dimension to the character of Phaedra. The audience knows that, although Hippolytus is said to disdain all women equally, in the words Aricia's confidante Ismene:

"Your first encounter much affected him…
His plaintive eyes betray his frigid mouth."

We know that Aricia has undermined Hippolytus' rejection of women, that he is responding romantically to her. Phaedra does not know this. Initially, because believing with Oenone that Hippolytus "has a fatal hatred of our sex", Phèdre boasts that she will have no rivals for the body of Hippolytus. Phèdre's discovery that "Aricia has his heart and only she" comes at the moment when she is preparing to contradict the story that Oenone gave Theseus of his son's lust for his stepmother and to tell him the truth, thus absolving Hippolytus. But, hearing of his affection for Aricia, jealousy kicks in and she does a volte-face. She admits that she cannot stand their happiness and wishes to crush Aricia, curses Oenone and moves nearer to suicide. "Why should I then have thought of his defence?" she asks rhetorically and only has the truth-telling meeting with Theseus after the death of Hippolytus. So, yes, on her deathbed, Phèdre does come clean: there is, as in the other plays, a late triumph for honesty and the truth of things. I think Phèdre retains our sympathies, but her jealousy makes her more complex, more human – more interesting.

Aricia is the powerful new added dimension that Racine adds to the dramatising of the Phaedra myth. Latterly she does not buckle when Theseus claims that Hippolytus intended to make her only his courtesan. "Can you not tell the good and bad apart?" she asks Theseus and her insistence on the goodness in Hippolytus leads Theseus to question his own judgment and the doom he has predicated on his son – too late, of course. In bringing out hitherto hidden character traits in Hippolytus, Phèdre and Theseus, Aricia's role in Racine's play is crucial. And she is nowhere to be found in either Euripides' or Seneca's play.

She also makes the psychological point about Theseus: "Your hands have freed mankind/From awful monsters of most every kind/And yet not all were slain." The monsters and demons within his own breast lead him to banish and send to his death his own son, believing the innocence of the "just" Phèdre. In the Second Scene of the Fourth Act the exchange between Theseus and Hippolytus is electrifying. The grieving father sees his son as infamous and a traitor, trying to wriggle out of the situation in which "just Phèdre (has) charmed your lewd eyes." He rejects him with the words: "Go find some friends who honour incest, who applaud adultery", ingrates and traitors who "rebel against the laws and dignity."

As in the other plays Theseus is full of grief and contrition at the end, and was affected by Aricia, but it is Hippolytus, being reasonable, who comes out of the exchanges with his father with a retained dignity. His final comment to his father is to point out that "your Phèdre is from a lineage and a mother who did horrors worse than any I could do." And before this he has been the voice of calm and reason, pointing out that everyone else sees the heart of Hippolytus as "pure as light of day", that he is the victim of a black lie. Tellingly he argues that he should be judged by "who I am and by the life I've led" and he points out – for me, a totally convincing argument – that "crime, like virtue, has degree.

> You never see pure shyness leap into
> The foul licentiousness you'd have me do."

The character of Hippolytus is so refreshingly different in Racine's play. No more is he the self-righteous, arrogant disdainer of women. We are in a world of much more complex characterisation, a more thoughtful, less black and white world. A modern world?

Yet as well as drawing on the subject matter of the Greek myths, Racine also adheres to Aristotle's rules of time and place with regard to tragedy. So that, whereas his theme of a failed and ineluctable struggle with the passions (the sex drive in the case of *Phèdre*), is both eternal and contemporary, there is a good deal that is **not** modern about Racine's plays. To some extent in the sixteen hundred or so years between the plays of Seneca and those of Racine little has changed – the myth remains essentially the same, uncontrollable passion presents distressing problems – but there really is this greater emphasis on character and the presentation of lust as a real **human** problem: with Racine each character has a past but the emphasis is on the independence that each character hopes (s)he has, believing that (s)he is free to act independently in the present. The Chorus has departed from *Phèdre* so there are no resonating bites of generalised wisdom for us to ponder. The audience may still despair at the human condition, but it is interaction of character that dominates. Noting that Euripides brought up what could be called feminist issues and Seneca's lurid violence prefigures Jacobean tragedy – to which topics we will return – it is time to take a step back in time and look at Faustus as a tragic figure.

But what wonderful plays are all three of those stemming from the Phaedra myth. Especially with regard to moving from the externalisation (whereby there is a possibility of guiltlessness and therefore acceptance and forgiveness) of a libido out of control to the internal acceptance that this non-ego-respecting sex drive can in itself be our fatal flaw. What do I do with my lust, ma?[4]

1. There is a play *Phaedra's Love* written by Sarah Kane in 1975, but it is —probably deliberately — a totally insensitive reworking and crude violation of the Phaedra myth. It shows a wilfully perverted incomprehension of the myth — and of Hippolytus in particular.
2. The minotaur was half man and half bull, feeding on human flesh — sacrificial youths and maidens.
3. It is arguable that, since Les Dawson, it is now mothers-in-law who have usurped step-mothers as the automatically vilified figures in the popular mind. Perhaps, though, they share a parity in notoriety.
4. Echoes of Melanie's *What have they done to my song, ma?*

CHRISTOPHER MARLOWE:
Doctor Faustus

Myths survive because they express eternal truths: they tap into the psyches of us all and we, with the blood of all human experience flowing in our veins, respond. With the possible exception of the Jesus myth, no story resonates more than the Faust myth. The story as we know it was first developed towards the end of the fourteenth century in Germany. Faustus – the name referencing the Latin for the chosen one or the special one, which of course also references the hubristic Jose Mourinho, manager of Chelsea Football Club – was a name adopted by many necromancers, but it is now believed that the origins of the story of the man who sold his soul to the devil lie with Georgius Faustus Helmstetensis who was expelled from the town of Ingolstadt for necromancy. Marlowe knew the story from the 1592 *The English Faust* book. I am going to use the first text we have of the play, the 1604 Quarto text, but the play was recordedly performed twenty-five times between October 1594 and October 1597. A popular play, though it is unlikely that one of its attractions was the possibility of seeing live devils on stage as William Prynne claimed had happened in his 1632 diatribe against the drama *Histriomastix*.

I find Marlowe's play of the scholar dissatisfied with all his learning and wanting to explore the outer bounds of knowledge fascinating, but before we look at his play I think it important that I mention other workings of the myth. There are many, including the 1963 *An Irish Faustus* by one of the great twentieth century novelists Lawrence Durrell, in which Faustus instructs Margaret of Galway in "science and magic", claiming to be teaching her only what she knows without being aware of, the unknown known. But there are two outstanding claimants for alternative Faustus-myth exploring: Goethe and Thomas Mann, both Germans as befits the original source of the myth.

Goethe's mind was occupied by Faust for most of his working life: he kept revisiting and reworking the drama and when he had finished it he died (1832) and it was published posthumously. Goethe's *Faust* is in two parts. Part One begins in Heaven, where we learn that Faust is God's favourite human being and Mephistophilis bets God that he can lure Faust away from his scholarly pursuits. In the next scene we see Faust fed up with orthodox learning in his ivory tower and turning to magic. So he is absolutely ripe for responding to the overtures of Mephistophilis who initially appears to him as a poodle. Faust signs away his life in blood – for current freedom to experience, with the assistance of Mephistophilis, everything he fancies; the payback for this is that at the end of his life he will serve the devil in hell. The main use of this opportunity given by the pact is the acquiring of an attractive village girl, Gretchen (or Margaret), whom he seduces, makes pregnant and then attempts to free her from prison where she is condemned to death for murdering her newly born illegitimate son. Faust's attitude towards Gretchen has changed from the initial lust of saying to Mephistophilis "Listen, you must get me the girl" to love. (Gretchen's mother and brother, though, both die as a result of her liaison with Faust.) Certainly she engenders compassion in Faust and a voice from heaven concludes the play with the promise that she will be saved, overruling Mephistophilis's "She is condemned to die."

In Part Two Faust has left the Gretchen experience behind. To a large extent that was a parochial exploration of the possibilities wrought by the relationship with Mephistophilis. Now he is granted the magic licence to range over myth and history, most notably seen in his achieving an idyllic marriage to Helen of Troy. At the end Faustus goes to Heaven, a recipient of divine mercy: "He who strives on and lives to strive/Can earn redemption still." In so far as Faust like Gretchen is saved, the ending of Part Two mirrors the ending of Part One, but in fact in Part Two Goethe has produced a play of philosophical and theological probing and questioning about man's defining characteristic – activity? Part One has a greater theatre history than Part Two, though both are infrequently performed, but as poetic presentations of great philosophical issues they have few rivals.

Whereas both Marlowe and Goethe have written works in dramatic form about Faust, Thomas Mann's work is in the form of a novel. I have chosen to comment on it here because it significantly brings the Faustus myth into the modern world. Mann has claims to being the greatest German novelist of all in so far as in a respected list of the best twentieth century German novels there are three[1] of his novels in the top ten. Be that as it may. What Mann does with the Faust theme is to have a musical composer, Adrian Leverkuhn, a man of great intellect and creative skills, wishing to achieve an outstanding level of greatness. To do this he contracts syphilis, thereby inducing madness and opening up all new channels of creativity. In his madness Leverkuhn sees a devil to whom he commits his soul in exchange for twenty-four years of genius. In fact he only has fourteen years of wonderful creativity before he has a breakdown and lives, cared for by relatives, in an infantile state for the remaining ten years of the pact. It is all a fascinating exploration of the process and demands of creativity. Parallel with this personal story Mann, through his narrator, Zeitblom, describes the growth and demise of the Nazi party and how it too sold its soul to the devil. As Leverkuhn ultimately, before his decline into infancy, kept creatively exploring the Apocalypse and the Last Judgment, we can see how Mann's novel works on many levels, with many theoretical strands tying it masterfully together. After Marlowe I find it the most rewarding of the Faust reworkings to read.

But it really is time we considered Marlowe's *Doctor Faustus*. The story is quite simple. Faustus is an eminent scholar in logic, medicine, law, philosophy and theology and is dissatisfied in what they have yielded him. He seeks power, omnipotence, wishing to be a god on earth. In order to attain this he forswears all studies but magic and necromancy, grounded by the study of astrology. To do this he sells his soul to the devil, Lucifer, so that in exchange for twenty-four years of omnipotence on earth, with Lucifer's servant Mephistophilis at his command, Faustus will finally go to hell. The play explores Faustus' use of his power and his inner thoughts and doubts. There are some relief-giving comic scenes, written in prose. And there is some sublime verse.

The basic theme, though, is a universal one. Mere learning is insufficient for a full life. How do we, then, all find meaning in our existence and how, in order to meet our individual psychological needs, do we conduct ourselves. Faustus chose power – and any just glance at any political system anywhere in the world shows how corrupting that is. And right from the opening Chorus Marlowe informs us of the fate of Faustus, with the Icarus reference:

> "Til swollen with cunning, of a self-conceit,
> His waxen wings did mount above his reach."

Hubris is Faustus' malady. Having listed his studies and his deep involvement with them, he laments: "Yet art thou still Faustus, and a man." So he is completely desirous of being ravished by magic. He wants everything that moves between heaven and earth to be at his command.

> "A sound magician is a mighty god;
> Here, Faustus, try thy brains to gain a deity."

And Faustus signs his pact with Lucifer in blood – though he could have heeded the warning by the blood of his cut arm being miraculously staunched, requiring Mephistophilis to open the wound with hot coals to finally effect the signing. But there was no heeding for Faustus.

Nor did he heed the warning of Mephistophilis. Eloquently Mephistophilis presents the case for Faustus to desist in his devilish quest for power and to be as a god:

> "Why, this is hell, nor am I out of it.
> Think'st thou that I, who saw the face of God,
> And tasted the eternal joys of heaven,
> Am not tormented with ten thousand hells,
> In being deprived of eternal bliss?
> Oh, Faustus, leave these frivolous demands,
> Which strike a terror to my fainting soul."

Such a plea would certainly have won me over. Not so Faustus. True, he struggles with the issues of salvation and damnation, both within himself through soliloquy and through the externalisation of this struggle represented by the Good and Evil Angels, but ultimately he chooses magic and power.

So how does he use this power for which he has sold his soul? Politicians at the very least pay lip service to using their exercise of power for the public good. Faustus, though, is exclusively selfish. He ignores the warning from Mephistophilis and when Lucifer shows him the seven deadly sins he dismisses them all to hell, without realising that they will be his companions when he too descends there. (For me the most intriguing sin is Envy, who declares: "I cannot read, and therefore wish all books were burnt.") When Jesus is taken to the top of a high mountain and tempted, he rejects the lure of power over all: Faustus, taken to the top of Olympus, succumbs. His first request, rather like Goethe's Faust, is to have a wife "the fairest maid in Germany, for I am wanton and lascivious." Mephistophilis derides any concept of marriage, and promises that:

> "I'll cull thee out the fairest courtesans,
> And bring them every morning to thy bed."

I accept that that is not an unattractive proposition, but one expects more from the scholar Faustus.

But more is what we do not get. He is taken to see the Pope and has fun at the Pontiff's expense by snatching the dish and cup from him as he is about to eat and drink. Then he boxes his ears, beats the attendant Friars and concludes by throwing fireworks amidst the Pope and his companions. A naughty thirteen year old might think this great fun – but Faustus, the great scholar, who now is an expert in astrology and much admired thereby? What he also does is to conjure up spirits resembling Alexander the Great and "his beauteous paramour" for the Emperor Carolus the Fifth and for himself Faustus has Mephistophilis conjure up "in twinkling of an eye" Helen of Troy. Faustus kisses her, but, more memorably, it is here we have an example of some of Marlowe's sublime verse:

> "Was this the face that launched a thousand ships,
> And burnt the topless towers of Ilium?
> Sweet Helen, make me immortal with a kiss."

But even as he is kissing Helen and commenting that "All is dross that is not Helena", he is aware that her lips are sucking forth his soul.

Faustus is constantly aware of the loss of his soul and the need to repent, but "sweet pleasure conquered deep despair." And the other pleasure he celebrates?

> "Have I not made blind Homer sing to me…
> Made music with my Mephistophilis."

All done through "divine astrology." Again memorable verse, but pure self-indulgence.

It should be noted too that Faustus, via Mephistophilis, brings the Duchess of Vanholt the "best grapes that e'er I tasted in my life". Otherwise we see the shallowness of this astrology-based necromancy when Robin the ostler and his friend Ralph, having stolen one of Faustus' conjuring books, fantasise about enjoying Nan Spit the kitchen-maid, before Mephistophilis frightens them by setting squibs at their backs. And Faustus employs his powers to humiliate a Knight by fixing on him a pair of cuckold's horns and also making a laughing stock of a horse-courser by selling him a horse for forty dollars and then turning it into a bottle of hay.

It is all very silly. One would hope for so much more from an intelligent, variously learned man with twenty-four years in which to exercise all the power in the world. Maybe if one had a mere twenty-four hours to live, knowing that in that limited time world-wonders are impossible, the selfish gene might justifiably kick in: you might opt for the best steak in the world or having sex with the widow next door or you might just contemplate your navel. Fair enough – but with twenty-four years one would expect sights to be set much higher: ridding the world of arms and armaments, ending global poverty – or, at least, poverty in Germany – and so on. In the selfish shallowness of his use of unlimited power, Faustus reveals the inadequacies of his priorities and the paucity of his philosophy.

Yet this perhaps also identifies him in the role of everyman. Maybe I am being a smug holier-than-thou in my disparagement of Faustus. Certainly Faustus is not the simplistic pleasure-seeker and mocker of pretence that I have thus far depicted. For there is a constant internal dialogue going on with himself, a dialogue about God and salvation. Confidently he initially dedicates himself to Belzebub: "There is no chief but Belzebub" and he boasts that he is not terrified by damnation. Yet before he signs his pact with Lucifer with his blood, alone in his study, we hear him wavering and admitting: "The god thou servest is thine own appetite." Within Faustus there is a constant realisation that repentance could produce salvation: "Christ did call upon the thief upon the cross." At one moment an Old Man assures him that:

"I see an angel hovers o'er thy head,
And, with a vial full of precious grace."

The Second Scholar encourages him to "look up to heaven (and) remember God's mercies are infinite." The Good Angel assures him that it is never too late "if Faustus can repent."

All this Faustus knows full well – he has, after all, been a professor of theology. He talks of repentance, but cannot honestly commit himself to it. He talks of renouncing his magic and repenting but then admits that "My heart's so hardened, I cannot repent." It's as though his intellectual rigour, brought about by his previous, unsatisfactory, disciplined scholarship compel Doctor Faustus to keep to the pact he has made with Lucifer. He knows he is damned and he despairs. But hell is his lot and desert. We hear, but Faustus does not, Mephistophilis' comment "His faith is great; I cannot touch his soul." God and his loss of heaven are never far from Faustus' ruminations. But he is scrupulously honest: even in his last hour and in his last speech Faustus knows that half a drop of Christ's blood would save him and he speaks of leaping up to his God, but something pulling him down. Repentance can never be total for "Faustus' offence can ne'er be pardoned … Lucifer and Mephistophilis. Ah …I gave them my soul for my cunning… for vain pleasure of twenty-four years hath Faustus lost eternal joy and felicity." And so at his end devils carry him off to hell.

It is a fate which Faustus, acknowledging how he has wasted his power in trivial pursuits, believes he deserves. Yet, could he have been saved – and **should** he have been saved? This is the central religious (and moral) issue of the play. An extra dimension is added to this discussion by contemporary Calvinist doctrine. Calvinism in Elizabethan England was a growing theological belief, dominating the intellectual thinking of the Church of England. Central to Calvinism was the belief in predestination: that an all powerful and all controlling God chooses who will be saved and who will be damned – our destiny is determined from the moment of our birth and there is nothing we can do about it. It's the "Che sara, sara"[2] that Faustus quotes as he rejects the study of divinity early in the play. God chooses his Elect, and by rejecting God and failing to repent we know that Faustus was never one of God's Elect. In many ways Faustus' sins are the greatest of all: he knows what God offers and rejects it. But really he was damned from the word go. What *Doctor Faustus* demonstrates is Calvin's "three-tiered concept of causation"[3], as his damnation is first willed by God, then by

Satan and finally by Faustus himself. Marlowe was a Cambridge University student and undoubtedly would have passed many small hours of the morning discussing such topics. This Calvinist aspect adds another dimension to discussion of the play and the merits of Faustus' damnation. Personally I think that, if we consider the play theologically – pace Calvin – Faustus is worthy of salvation, but if we consider it from a human and moral perspective his damnation is warranted.

Be that as it may. What I hope I have demonstrated is that in *Doctor Faustus*, working with one of the great myths, Marlowe has given us a play for all seasons as he explores theological dilemma and human turpitude. He opens up the issue of how power is used by humans too. And there is some wonderful verse. There may be some comic scenes that a twenty-first century audience struggle to respond to, but all in all the play is a fascinating recreation of the central myth of selling your soul for power, and what then to do with that power. Intellectual studies and scholarship proved ultimately unsatisfactory to Doctor Faustus. But what **does** guarantee satisfaction?

---

[1] It is a list compiled by German writers and scholars. *Doctor Faustus* is at number 10. Mann's *The Magic Mountain* is at number 3 and his *Buddenbrooks* at number 7. The list is topped by Robert Musil's *The Man Without Qualities* and Kafka has two entries.

[2] Or, in the words of Doris Day *"Que Sera sera."*

[3] John Stachniewski: *The Persecutory Imagination: English Puritanism and the Literature of Religious Despair.* OUP 1991.

SHAKESPEARE

I hope I have established that tragedy is the art form that engages with all the major issues of life: freedom and fate; revenge and forgiveness; knowledge and the purpose and meaning of life. What Shakespeare explores in his major tragedies are the psychological drives and dilemmas that beset mankind. In plays such as *Romeo and Juliet* and *Antony and Cleopatra* he presents characters driven to extremes by the overwhelming power of love, and with *Titus Andronicus* he demonstrates his interest in the revenge theme. But what I want to focus on are the four major tragedies: *Hamlet* (1601), *Othello* (1603), *King Lear* (1605) and *Macbeth* (1606). In these plays he explores: the Oedipal complex and madness; envy, jealousy and racism; old age and the loss of power, parent-child relations and madness; ruthless ambition and loyalty respectively. Themes for today and every day.

Freud, of course, used *Hamlet* as a classic example of the Oedipal complex – Oedipus loving Jocasta was not an isolated event! Freud's argument is that Hamlet is jealous of his uncle's having usurped (by murder) his father in his mother's bed. Freud argues that Hamlet's uncle, Claudius, has done what all boys want to do – kill their father and marry their mother. This is not the place to evaluate the validity of Freud's theory, but there is no doubting Hamlet's abhorrence of his mother's behaviour when he speaks of her living "in the rank sweat of an enseamed bed/Stewed in corruption, honeying and making love/Over the nasty sty." Previously he had noted the dexterity with which she had hastened to "incestuous sheets." For Hamlet there is a natural disgust at his mother's brazen sexual behaviour. This disgust and confusion transfers itself towards his behaviour to his girlfriend Ophelia. Yet, ignored by Freudians, there is the rejection of his mother's sexuality: "You cannot call it love, for at your age/The heyday in the blood is tame, it's humble/And waits upon the judgment."

The point is that Hamlet is confused and out of his depth. *Hamlet* is a revenge play too. He is a Wittenberg University student who is beseeched by the ghost of his dead father to revenge his untimely death: action rather than words are required, and Hamlet is a man of words. Let me give a brief outline of the story. The night watch on the ramparts of the castle in Elsinore have seen what appears to be the ghost of the late king of Denmark, an indication that "something is rotten in the state of Denmark." They invite his son, through his friend Horatio, to watch with them on the following night. The ghost appears again and has a private dialogue with Hamlet: it is his father's ghost and the ghost entrusts Hamlet with revenging his "murder most foul", committed by his own brother who now is married to the queen Gertrude. The horror of what he has heard appals Hamlet. Revenge is certainly justified, but Hamlet is a university student. He possesses skills as a fencer, but he is a scholar too. So there is much soliloquising and heart-searching about killing his uncle. Horrified too by his mother's hasty remarriage, he uses two strategies to delay the revenge: he has strolling players enact, with a part written in by Hamlet himself, a representation of his father's murder – and the new King, Claudius, seemingly reveals his guilt, by walking out before the conclusion of the play. The other strategy that Hamlet employs is to feign madness – disturbed, as he is, this is not difficult.

Hamlet is in a relationship with Ophelia, the daughter of Polonius, Denmark's Lord Chamberlain and chief minister. Perplexed and disgusted by his mother's bed-swopping, believing "frailty thy name is woman", Hamlet rejects Ophelia, telling her "to get thee to a nunnery."[1].This contributes towards her later crazy behaviour and suicide by drowning. The other major contributory factor is that Hamlet kills her father: in an intimate scene in which he confronts and upbraids his mother in her bedroom, Hamlet hears a sound from behind an arras, and, believing it to be the king, stabs the person hiding behind the arras. It was Ophelia's father Polonius. After this Hamlet accepts the fate of being sent to England on behalf of Denmark. He is accompanied by two fellow students from Wittenberg, Rosencranz and Guildenstern, who have been spying on him at the behest of Claudius. Hamlet is to give letters to the King of England, which, unknown to Hamlet, instruct the English king to put Hamlet to death "for like the hectic in my blood he rages." Hamlet, en voyage, discovers these instructions, and rewrites the letter asking that Rosencranz and Guildenstern be killed. And then the ship in which he is travelling is attacked by pirates and Hamlet taken on board and returned by the pirates to Denmark.

On Danish soil he comes across the discreet burial of Ophelia. Her brother, Laertes, is there, and Hamlet broils with him in her grave, declaring his love for her –"Forty thousand brothers/Could not with all their quality of love/Make up the sum." This antagonism between Laertes, who blames Hamlet for his father and sister's deaths, is used by Claudius: he arranges a duel between them, but he has the tip of Laertes' sword envenomed with deadly poison and, in the event of this not working, has a poisoned chalice prepared. In the ensuing fencing match, Hamlet is fatally wounded, swords are exchanged and thereby Laertes is also fatally wounded. The queen drinks to Hamlet and dies. As do both Laertes and Hamlet, but not before Laertes confesses the king's plot, enabling Hamlet to, finally, exact his father's revenge and kill Claudius, with both the envenomed sword and the poisoned chalice.

That is a long story, and it is by far Shakespeare's longest play. And I have not mentioned Fortinbras. He is a military parallel to the student Hamlet. Fortinbras reappears at the end of the play and has the vote of Hamlet's "dying voice" to rule Denmark. He is a prince of Norway, and we have previously seen him swaggering with his army, leading them for the conquest of a small piece of pretty worthless land. Thus the military commander is contrasted with the intellectual Hamlet[2] who dithers about one simple act of revenge justice. It is, of course, debatable, whether the attributes possessed by Fortinbras make him more fit to rule than Hamlet.

I used the word "dithers" provocatively. The generally accepted reading of Hamlet's behaviour is that he is intelligently weighing up the pros and cons of a revenge killing – but this does mean, as Hamlet accepts, "conscience[3] does make cowards of us all." This weighing up is experienced by the audience in terms of Hamlet's soliloquies. Everybody knows the suicide contemplation of the "To be or not to be" speech, but the play is full of introspection: "O that this too sullied flesh would melt", "Oh, what a rogue and peasant slave am I!", "How all occasions do inform against me" are all meaningful contemplative arias. There is Hamlet's reflection too on the nature of mankind: "What a piece of work is a man, how noble in reason, how infinite in faculties… the beauty of the world, the paragon of animals…" This is a serious man, with a serious view on the world, casting doubts on the morality of revenge killing, and, through his soliloquies we, the audience, are privy to the workings of his mind. It is the mind of someone who, in Ophelia's view has been a courtier, scholar, soldier and perfectly mannered fashionista. And now he has lost it: Ophelia laments "O what a noble mind is here o'erthrown!" We the audience follow Hamlet's reasoning and dilemma all the way through the play: this is what I mean by the opening up of psychological dilemmas which Shakespeare brings to the theatre.

Of course he brings much more too – in particular the breadth of understanding of pretty well all human behaviour and some of the most sublime verse. In *Hamlet*, as later in *The Tempest*, there is in addition a focus on the revenge theme. In the end Hamlet simply accepts his destiny:

"There's a divinity that shapes our ends,
Rough-hew them how we will",

whereas Prospero in the later play, prompted by Ariel, makes a decision that "The rarer action is/In virtue than in vengeance." But the engaging of sympathy for Hamlet, so that the audience is with him and his indecision every breath of the way, is what ultimately makes *Hamlet* a great play.

Something very similar can be said about *Othello*. Once Iago's constant feeding of Othello's insecurity has worked its way indelibly into Othello's mind, he shares with us his thoughts about what he perceives (entirely wrongly) to be his wife's infidelity and what he should do about it. Another similarity between Hamlet and Othello is that, along with Macbeth, but not with King Lear, they have not quite reached the position of eminence from which, in his writings about tragedy, Aristotle wanted his tragic heroes to fall: Hamlet is a prince and king in waiting, Othello the general has undoubtedly done great military service on behalf of the Venetian republic, and Macbeth is also a great military servant of the Scottish King but is not in line for the succession. None of these three rule – which probably increases the likelihood of you and me being able to identify with them and sympathise. But as well as their steep descent from grace and their, through soliloquy, sharing their doubts and dilemmas with us the audience, what also gives the plays heft is their presentation of an all too common human predicament. With Hamlet it was how to respond to the murder of his father and his mother's "o'er hasty marriage." With Othello it all revolves around jealousy, when you believe that the woman you love is granting sexual favours to others.

Briefly, the story of *Othello*. The first Act is set in Venice. The Senate has heard that a Turkish fleet is sailing to Cyprus with a view to conquering this Venetian possession. Venice's most successful military commander, Othello, is sent for to take charge of the garrison in Cyprus and defeat the planned Turkish invasion. Othello, though, the black African outsider, has wooed with his tales of derring-do and subsequently secretly married the white Desdemona. At such a match between an "old black ram" who is "tupping" his "white ewe" Desdemona's father is horrified and brings his complaint to the Senate. The Duke of Venice, having heard Othello's story, believes him, that no witchcraft was involved in the wooing, and dismisses the complaint. Brabantio, Desdemona's father, abandons her and Othello and Desdemona set sail, in separate ships, for Cyprus.

The last four Acts all take place in Cyprus. In fact three ships set out from Venice to Cyprus. The main person in the other ship is Iago. He has actually set up the plot of the play in the very first scene when he confesses to Roderigo that he is envious of Cassio, having been promoted above him to be Othello's deputy when he Iago has seen so much fighting alongside Othello, whereas Cassio is a mere "arithmetician", a theorist. He also has a vague suspicion that Othello has slept with his "nightcap", his wife Emilia, Desdemona's companion. For these reasons Iago is awaiting an opportunity to have revenge on Othello, and Roderigo, a Venetian nobleman, hopelessly in love with Desdemona, is recruited to accompany Iago to Cyprus on the promise of eventually enjoying Desdemona.

Stormy seas ensure that there is some doubt as to whether the three ships will safely make it to Cyprus. But they do arrive, though the same stormy seas have sunk the Turkish fleet, so there is no longer any military threat. Plenty of time for Iago to plan the demise of Othello. By a number of subtle ways, mainly involving a dream falsely related and a lost strawberry-marked handkerchief, Iago implies that Desdemona is being unfaithful with Cassio. Othello takes the bait and his jealousy is such that he has a brief fit and is never in his right mind from then onwards. His tortured mind, though, dictates that he kill Cassio and Desdemona. In fact in a scuffle it is Roderigo, still working for Iago on a false promise, who is killed, though Othello succeeds in suffocating Desdemona. The truth dawns on Emilia that her husband is behind the rumours and killings and she denounces him. Iago stabs Emilia fatally and thus, too late, silences her; he then vows that, even under torture, "From this time forth I never will speak word." Othello, beside himself with grief and self-rage stabs himself to death.

Just as Hamlet the thinking man is out of his depth and comfort zone when it comes to having been summonsed to revert to the barbarism of killing, so Othello is similarly discombobulated when, out of his sphere of knowledge and expertise, he is confronted with daily living in a white society in which he is totally unfamiliar with the rules and norms. This ignorance makes him wide open to Iago's wiles. In the first place he knows he is not good-looking by Venetian standards – even Desdemona clarifies his attraction to her with "I saw Othello's visage in his mind." And he himself acknowledges the sexual revulsion the Venetians have for black on white sex by asserting that he is old enough to be no longer heated by lust and that he has married Desdemona "to be free and bounteous to her mind." The wonderful catalogue of military prowess with which he won Desdemona has left him no time for amorous pursuits. The threatened Turkish fleet having been dispersed to the four winds, Othello has lost his purpose and function in Cyprus. He has been freed to centre on his marriage with Desdemona, and is clearly out of his depth.

So when Iago, talking of women, asserts that:

> "In Venice they do let God see the pranks
> They dare not show their husbands; their best conscience
> Is not to leave undone, but keep unknown…"

Othello accepts women's infidelity as standard behaviour. Gullible in the extreme, he credulously believes Iago's suggestions of Desdemona's infidelity with Cassio. It is true that twice in Act 3 Scene 3 Othello demands "proof" from Iago. The "proofs" – a dream and a misplaced handkerchief – would not have begun to be seen as valid evidence in a court of law, but to a jealous, sexually tortured mind almost anything vaguely relevant feeds in to the irrational conviction. Once Othello has the picture of Desdemona's infidelity in his mind he cannot rid himself of it. That thought and picture induce a fit in him. He does not want to know, but once he knows, led by the green eyed monster, the only way to banish the horror of Desedmona's imagined sexual liaisons is to eliminate Desdemona:

> "I had been happy if the general camp,
> Pioneers and all, had tasted her sweet body,
> So had I nothing known."

He strikes her in public and then smothers her fatally in the sheets of their wedding night bed. He blathers on about doing it for "the cause" and "lest she betray more men", but by now not only has his beloved "reputation" gone, so has his rational thinking – completely gone.

Reputation, occupation, rationality, dignity, all of Othello's best attributes, all have been lost by the end of the play. He retrieves some dignity in his final speech –"Soft you, a word or two before you go"– but we the audience have witnessed the decline of a great and dignified military leader. Iago's "mischief" has worked and Othello has murdered, in Emilia's words, "the sweetest innocent that e'er did lift up eye." And yet, and yet, our sympathy goes out to Othello.

There are two ways Shakespeare achieves this. One is through the portrait of the truly Machiavellian Iago. He is a vicious and highly accomplished schemer. The socially inept Othello was putty in his hands. Not only does he destroy Othello (and, incidentally, his stooge Roderigo) he relishes the whole process. By the end of Act 3 Scene 3 he has achieved what he initially complained about: he has replaced Cassio as Othello's lieutenant, but this does not stop him continuing to undermine Othello's confidence. He has practised upon Othello's "peace and quiet even to madness" and this "honest, honest Iago" has succeeded in destroying the Moor, the man "of a constant, loving, noble nature". Which is exactly what he said he would do at the end of Act 2 Scene 1. The character of Iago demands a few thousand words to itself, but this is not in the brief of this discussion of tragedy! What is important here, though, is that, confronted with the skills of Iago, Othello never had a chance.

The other means Shakespeare uses to arouse our sympathy for Othello (and is also used to help follow the workings of Iago's mind) is through the same means he employed in *Hamlet*: that is through soliloquy. To be more accurate, there is far less soliloquy in *Othello* than there is in *Hamlet*, but there are a number of long speeches in which we see how Othello's mind is working: in the beginning of the play we have the dignified, explanatory speeches to the Senate and at the end a final dignity is just about achieved. In between we have the revealing dialogue with Iago in Act 3 Scene 3, the soliloquy of "this fellow's of exceeding honesty", the address to Desdemona of "Had it pleased heaven" and the "It is the cause, it is the cause, my soul" soliloquy all attesting to Othello's tortured thinking. Obviously there are shorter relevant speeches. The point is that we are privy to what motivates the character, and privy to his self-destructive doubts. To understand all is not necessarily to excuse all but it does evoke sympathy. That is one of Shakespeare's great achievements.

We must turn to the third play, chronologically, of Shakespeare's four great tragedies, *King Lear*. In *Hamlet* the issues of revenge and (to a much lesser extent) the frailty and unreliability of women are the issues explored via the dominant personality of Hamlet; in *Othello* there is also Iago's revenge motive, but it is Othello's tortured jealousy, made worse by his being an outsider by race and social position, that is the major theme explored. With *King Lear* we have yet more themes, developed further by a subplot, and again we are privy to the workings of the protagonist's mind. These themes – major by the standards of any society – revolve around the loss of power in old age, the parent/child relationship, the fear of madness and, what is increasingly a theme in Shakespeare's later plays, the need for forgiveness and reconciliation. In this latter context it is interesting that in *Othello* there is no semblance of the villainous Iago being reconciled with anyone, whereas in *Hamlet* there is a reconciliation between Hamlet and Laertes and in *King Lear* there is also a reconciliation between the bastard Edmund and his legitimate brother Edgar.

The story of *King Lear* is fairly straightforward. Lear is eighty years of age and he wishes to retire from kingship, dividing the kingdom into three, to be ruled over by his three daughters and their husbands. To determine who gets the most opulent share he asks for a declaration of love from these daughters. The two elder daughters, Goneril and Regan, gush their exaggerated affection and Lear is well pleased; his youngest and favourite daughter Cordelia cannot heave her heart into her mouth and points out – as did Desdemona to her father – that she is grateful to him for life but now her greater love would be to her husband. As Brabantio rejected Desdemona so Lear rejects Cordelia, and her third of the kingdom is shared between Goneril and Regan. Dowerless, Cordelia marries the King of France and leaves England with him.

Lear intends to alternate living – he and his hundred knights – between his other two daughters. But they refuse to accommodate his wishes, claiming that he no longer needs any knights to accompany him. So he is turned away from their houses and that of Gloucester and endures a night of thunderstorms, exposed to the elements. He is accompanied by a disguised Kent, who has been loyal to him despite what he sees as his mistreatment of Cordelia, his Fool, and Edgar the legitimate son of Gloucester who has been traduced by his bastard brother and is disguised as Poor Tom the beggar, feigning madness. It is a desperate and unlikely collection of people and Lear fears for his wits.

Gloucester is in touch with Cordelia and France, but communicates this to his illegitimate son Edmund and is then betrayed by him; with the result that Regan's husband Cornwall gouges out Gloucester's eyes and leaves him to wander outdoors, where the two betrayed fathers, Lear and Gloucester, touchingly meet up. Gloucester dies but is reconciled to his son Edgar at the last. And Lear too, an inch away from real madness, dies from grief when he realises that Cordelia has been hanged (on Edmund's orders); however, before that, the two have also been reconciled.

That's about it. Edmund has professed love to both Goneril and Regan. Both respond to Edmund – Regan is actually free to respond as her husband Cornwall was killed by a servant when the servant saw how horrifically Gloucester was treated – but their rivalry results in Goneril poisoning Regan and then taking her own life. Edmund is killed in a duel with Edgar, and the play ends with an unpromising triumvirate of the aged Kent, the legitimate son Edgar (Poor Tom the mad beggar) and Albany, the weak but fundamentally decent husband of Goneril, left to rule England.

On the surface Lear is a less than attractive hero: his demanding a public display of affection from his children is pitiful, as is his attaching rewards to manifestations of affection; his demand to keep the trappings of kingship with a retinue of a hundred knights is clearly unreasonable; and his vicious cursing of his daughters – he labels Regan "a boil, a plague-sore, or embossed carbuncle" and wishes sterility in the vilest terms on Goneril – illustrate the self-centred aggression that is characteristic of the Lear we initially meet.

And yet and yet and yet... Perhaps he is, as he claims, "a man more sinned against than sinning": he is subjected to a massive rejection by his two elder daughters. In old age, having given away his power, it is reasonable that a king (indeed all of us) should retain a measure of stature and standing, as, for Lear, exemplified by his knights. And to have no roof over your head on a stormy blasted heath is no picnic for anyone, let alone an eighty year old who fears for his sanity. The crucial line of the play, it seems to me, is Regan's early comment: "yet he hath ever but slenderly known himself." And what Shakespeare does is to take this initially unsympathetic tyrant and bring out his human qualities, so that, as we share Lear's journey, we appreciate his coming to understand himself and what matters in life for the first time – and so we finally feel for and sympathise with him.

Lear shares a good deal with the audience. True there is bluster and denunciation at the outset, but after the storm he has acquired an understanding of the nature of mankind without the superficial robes of power: he begins to realise what it is like to be one of "his poorest subjects" and that when it comes to "the great image of Authority/A dog's obeyed in office." "Robs and furred gowns" conceal the rich man's vices too. With Gloucester he may claim to be "every inch a king" but what in fact we have is someone who is every inch a human being.

This is what the true tragic hero does. King he may be, but he becomes a representation of everyman. A father (or mother) can experience "how sharper than a serpent's tooth it is to have a thankless child." Old age inevitably is accompanied by the fear of madness or some form of dementia. And when we no longer have a role in society, what do we do with our lives? As for downsizing a retinue, I guess most of us see this in terms of reducing our living space and then, certainly for me, what do I do with my thousands of books that have been my faithful companions throughout my life?

Life is not rational. We may not agree with Gloucester's despairing remark that "As flies to wanton boys are we to th'Gods/They kill us for their sport", but we can identify with Lear's "O! reason not the need" when he argues that there is more to the life of a man than having his basic needs met. We have, for example, instincts and insights: such an instinct Lear had that the bond between his youngest daughter Cordelia and himself was the strongest of all his family bonds. Finally he comes to recognise this, but if only at the outset he had acted on this instinct…

Of course had he done so we would not have had the magnificent play. When we leave the theatre we remember Lear's "pelican daughters", but overall we remember the trials and travails of "a very foolish, fond old man". Through his intimacy with the audience we have shared his journey from unthinking tyrant to compassionate human being – and a man who has seen through the humbug and pretension of people in authority. Despite the horrors in the first part of the play and the deaths at the conclusion, we take other positive values from *King Lear*: perhaps reconciliation and forgiveness are the strongest values, but there is also the matter of loyalty too, as evinced by Kent, Gloucester, Edgar, the Fool – and Cordelia. It really is a remarkable play.

Macbeth is a much shorter play, focusing mainly on the nature of ambition (and to a much lesser extent the basic rules of hospitality), but we now have two protagonists, Macbeth and Lady Macbeth, through whose eyes we experience the drama. Both reveal so much of the workings of their minds through soliloquy, Macbeth in particular: "Two truths are told…", "If it were done…", "Is this a dagger…", "To be thus…", "This push will cheer me…",

"Tomorrow, and tomorrow, and tomorrow…" – all take us inside the workings of Macbeth's mind. Then there is Lady Macbeth's "Glamis thou art" and some taut, dynamic dialogue between the two of them, all of which, by having shared their thinking, helps us understand their actions and thereby increases our sympathy.

For the outline of the story does not redound to either of their credits. What happens is this. The King of Scotland, Duncan, has employed two generals, Macbeth and Banquo, to defeat the invading Norwegian army; they succeed and Macbeth is rewarded by being made Thane of Cawdor, replacing the traitor who had assisted Norway. This fulfils a prophecy that had been made to Macbeth and Banquo by three witches they had met on a heath in thunder: they also prophesied that Macbeth would become King and that Banquo would be the father of Kings. Macbeth relays this news by letter to his wife and also immediately afterwards she hears that Duncan is coming to stay that night.

> "The raven himself is hoarse,
> That croaks the fatal entrance of Duncan
> Under my battlements"

soliloquises Lady Macbeth. She knows her husband is ambitious but is too full of the milk of human kindness to act ruthlessly to attain his ambitions. It is she who must gear him up to kill. And, despite Macbeth's protestations that he is both Duncan's kinsman and his host, her force of personality ensures that Macbeth, still full of doubt and fear, murders Duncan while he sleeps. For what they see as their own safety Duncan's sons, Malcolm and Donalbain, flee to England and Ireland respectively, but this flight enables Macbeth to suggest that they were guilty of killing their father. Macbeth is crowned King at Scone.

There follows a shift of power in the dynamics of the Macbeth/Lady Macbeth relationship. After killing Duncan, Macbeth had murdered the grooms attendant on their king. On hearing this unplanned development, Lady Macbeth faints and is never quite the same again – and we, towards the end of the play, meet her sleepwalking unable to wash the blood off her hands, and then we hear she has taken her own life. Macbeth has taken control – indeed as he plans to murder for his own security, he tells her to "be innocent of the knowledge, dearest chuck, till thou applaud the deed." He hires two murderers to eliminate Banquo and his son Fleance, hoping to nullify the witches' prophecy. Banquo is killed but Fleance escapes. And Macbeth is not rid of Banquo, for his ghost appears at the coronation banquet; only Macbeth can see him and in her last show of a little remaining power Lady Macbeth just about holds things together. But suspicions of Macbeth's guilt of murder grow. By now he is so far stepped in blood that he has to go on killing – for his security, as he thinks – and he has Macduff's wife and children killed.

This brings together Macduff and Duncan's elder son Malcolm and, abetted by the English king, they take an army to Scotland to dethrone Macbeth. In the meantime the witches have made three more prophecies to Macbeth, to beware Macduff, only to fear when Birnam Wood moves towards his castle at Dunsinane and that he is cannot be harmed by any "of woman born." Macbeth has no friends, his wife has committed suicide, but stoically he awaits the opposing army, trusting in the witches' so far fulfilled prophecies. Malcolm orders branches of trees to be cut from Birnam Wood to disguise the size of his advancing army and when, confronted face to face with Macduff, Macbeth learns that Macduff was "from his mother's womb untimely ripped", the end is a formality, but he does die fighting. Malcolm is crowned King and peace returns to a disturbed and perturbed country. And, finally, to fulfil the witches' prophecies Fleance eventually fathers future Scottish kings, amongst whom was Shakespeare's patron King James I of England, King James VI of Scotland.

There is a memorable comment made by Macbeth, when he is trying to dissuade himself from killing Duncan, about basic rules of hospitality: as host to Duncan, Macbeth "should against his murderer shut the door,/Not bear the knife myself." But the central issue raised by *Macbeth* is that of ambition. Before he heard from the witches we know that Macbeth had dreamed of being King, but his wife knows that he is also "too full o' the milk of human kindness/To catch the nearest way." Initially murder is not for him. But ambition – and Lady Macbeth – can change perspectives. So Macbeth murders Duncan, only to find that this does not bring the satisfaction he had hoped for. Parallels abound: the seekers after money, power, fame in the world today, once achieved, realise that these goals do not bring the satisfaction and contented security that they had imagined. I cannot envisage Tony Blair ever having a comfortable night's sleep.

It is Duncan who sleeps well in *Macbeth*; "after life's fitful fever he sleeps well." Macbeth, though, believes that he has murdered sleep and will sleep no more, and we witness his wife's apparently nightly sleepwalking. Shortly after the murder of Duncan she had simplistically claimed that "a little water clears us of this deed"; sleepwalking, she is for ever washing her hands and asserts that "all the perfumes of Arabia will not sweeten this little hand." For we are what we have been and what we have done: we cannot escape the consequences of our past actions. Macbeth has to continue wading through his river of blood; he cannot turn back. And he needs to feel secure, which means a constant programme of murdering those who are perceived to be his enemies – in every such house he has inserted a paid informer. Ambition, ruthlessly pursued, does not bring peace of mind and security: this is the theme profoundly explored in *Macbeth*.

It is a play of contrasting red and black: the red of the blood frequently referenced, and the black of darkness: "Light thickens… Good things of day begin to droop and drowse." Macbeth's mind is full of scorpions. There are many references to fear and to the clothes of kingship not fitting Macbeth.

I wish to conclude this long essay, though, by focusing on the psychological insights that Shakespeare brings to his characters, and thereby to us. Macbeth is beset by doubts about murder – left to his own devices it is certain that he would not have killed Duncan. It is his wife who spurs him on. A powerful, demanding woman, she asserts that she would have dashed her suckling child's brains out rather than renege on the promise of murder that Macbeth has made, and she taunts him with being less than a man if he fears to go through with killing Duncan. The dialogue between the two, the tension engendered by it, before Duncan's murder is almost unbearable – indeed before the discovery of Duncan's body, Shakespeare reduces the tension with a comic scene, with a porter imagining he is porter of Hell gate[4]… There is similar tension in the banquet scene when Macbeth is haunted by Banquo's ghost. These are two completely realised characters, and through the dynamics of their relationship and their soliloquies[5] we understand their motivations and their actions, her disintegration and his bravery at the last.

I make no apologies for writing about four Shakespeare plays. One reason is that an English speaking audience is more likely to see one of these plays than any other I have and will be writing about. The main reason, however, is that Shakespeare is an indisputable genius. I have scarcely mentioned the wonders of much of his verse, nor his breadth of compassion – those qualities are there in abundance. And so is this magnificent insight into the human mind and the depth of understanding he brings to the eternal issues he explores. Number 1 all-time playwright!

---

[1] A nunnery was also the slang term for a brothel.

[2] Hamlet has being studying at Wittenberg – though in reality not founded till 1508 – for years. David Warner was brilliant in the role of Hamlet in the Peter Hall production of 1965, playing Hamlet as a rust-red-scarfed university student.

[3] Conscience meaning "thinking too much".

[4] Interestingly the one servant loyal to Macbeth at the end is called Seyton.

[5] Banquo also soliloquises a good deal too.

JACOBEAN AND CAROLINE THEATRE
1603–1642

John Webster: *The Duchess of Malfi* (1613)
John Ford: *'Tis Pity She's a Whore* (1633)

There is a plethora of plays written in the early years of the seventeenth century, before Cromwell's Act of Parliament closed down the theatres on September 2nd 1642. Probably the four best known playwrights are John Webster, Thomas Dekker, Thomas Middleton and John Ford. I have passed over the Thomases in favour of the Johns, not because I hold a brief against Thomas, but because I think the two plays I have chosen are most likely to be staged today.[1] What the two plays have thematically in common is forbidden love – and how cruelly and viciously a conservative, establishment society responds to this. The terms Jacobean and Caroline are used simply to place them in the period of the reigns respectively of James 1 (1603–1625) and Charles 1 (1625–1642) – the terminology, though, is not important: I could equally well have used the words late Renaissance Theatre, a term applied to the English theatre from 1562 to 1642, when the theatre so flourished.

But – letting go of the history – let's turn to the plays. The first thing to say about these two plays is that they demonstratively are not Shakespearean in tone. Revenge plays were common in this period, and Shakespeare's early revenge play *Titus Andronicus* is a pretty violent, cruel drama[2], but by the time he further explores the possibility of revenge, in *Hamlet* and *The Tempest*, a more introspective calm and wisdom have taken over. Ultimately, I believe, we find Shakespeare's greatness not only in his poetry, but also in his compassionate understanding of human behaviour. With Webster especially we have some memorable poetry, but in both plays compassion is a commodity hard to come by. Amongst all the intrigue and distrust, the need to revenge breeds what is pretty much an exultancy in violence, torture and bloody punishment.

Compassion and understanding have fled. No, Shakespeare it is not!

The story of *The Duchess of Malfi* is as follows. The Duchess is a widow, following the death of her older husband, the Duke of Malfi. Her elder brother, a Cardinal, and her twin brother Ferdinand feel they have the right to control whom she next marries – and indeed forbid her to remarry, fearing a dilution of their inheritance. In fact the Duchess effects a clandestine marriage to her chief steward Antonio. They are happy and she bears three children. An ex-con Bosola is employed by the Duchess as the manager of her horses, but in reality is more significantly employed as a spy for the Cardinal and Ferdinand. Her marriage to Antonio discovered, the Duchess concocts a story that Antonio has run off with her jewels and has fled. In the meantime she goes on a pilgrimage to Our Lady of Loretto, on the advice of Bosola; this shrine being "scarce seven leagues from fait Ancona" where Antonio will be waiting for her. Bosola tells the Cardinal of the plan. Antonio escapes, but the Duchess and her two younger children are returned to Malfi and, under Ferdinand's instructions, are murdered.

Meanwhile the Cardinal murders his mistress Julia by means of a poisoned Bible and intends to kill Bosola, for he too, like Julia, knew too much. Bosola overhears the Cardinal's intentions and goes to murder him but, in error in the dark, kills Antonio. He then stabs the Cardinal to death, and in a subsequent brawl Bosola and Ferdinand kill each other. The play concludes with the eldest son of the Duchess and Antonio, somehow having survived the mayhem, being proclaimed as heir to the Dukedom and consequent fortune of Malfi.

What this outline does not do justice to is the characterisation of the Duchess and her two brothers. Their characters are clearly delineated, though their defining characteristics remain constant throughout. The most complex character is Bosola, who changes through experience. But more of this later!

Thwarted love is an eternal theme. There is no doubting the love between the Duchess and Antonio. It is the Duchess who makes the running: as she points out: "The misery of us that are born great/We are forced to woo." But she is not pulling rank in her wooing of the honest, virtue-serving Antonio: "…(I) only do appear to you, a young widow/That claims you for her husband." The Duchess's attendant woman Cariola sees this marriage as showing "a fearful madness", and Antonio too wonders about her brothers' reaction, only to be assured that "time will easily scatter the tempest."

Unfortunately the Duchess is completely wrong. She and Antonio are not free to love. As she later laments:

"The birds, that live i'the field
On the wild benefit of nature, live
Happier than we; for they may choose their mates,
And carol their sweet pleasures to the spring."

I have mentioned her brothers' opposition to the marriage as being based on their wanting their share of her inherited wealth, but this in not the only reason for their disapproval of their sister's behaviour. The Cardinal is also concerned that "the royal blood of Aragon and Castile be thus attainted" and had previously warned his sister that with a secret marriage "the marriage night is the entrance into some prison." It is somewhat more complicated when it comes to Ferdinand. I will talk about his reputation vis-à-vis the law and his lycanthropy and madness later, but in the context of his sister it is true to say that he lusts after her himself. In Act 2 Scene 1, lines 255–256, he makes an overtly sexual reference and later has a fantasy that she is with "some strong-thighed bargeman." There is a madness and a jealousy about him. The lovers did not stand a chance.

It is difficult to find fault with the Duchess and Antonio. I suppose there is an element of blasphemy involved in a shrine being employed in their plan to deceive the brothers[3], and there are certainly echoes of Ferdinand's calling his sister "a notorious strumpet" when we hear the "common rabble do directly say she is a strumpet", but this is when the marriage is still a secret, and is on account of its having been noticed how Antonio has had preferment and grown rich. However, we have the witness of Antonio, talking at length to his friend Delio in Act 1 Scene 2, about the wonderful qualities of the Duchess: "her days are practised in such noble virtue" and much more. She is a strong woman too in so far as she refuses to kowtow to her brothers' wishes, which in a male dominated society is laudable. Love, not financial reward, is the basis of her decision making. The closing couplet of the play are said by Delio:

> "Integrity of life is fame's best friend,
> Which nobly, beyond death, shall crown the end."

A fair comment on the Duchess.

I do not wish to give the impression, though, that *The Duchess of Malfi* is character-driven. It is the atmosphere of cruelty and corruption that pervades. Ferdinand wishes to drive the Duchess mad: he uses wax figurines to deceive her into believing that Antonio is dead, and he frees mad folk from the hospital to sing and dance and gambol outside her mansion at night to deprive his sister of sleep. Corruption is best seen in the Cardinal. As well as being jointly responsible for hiring Bosola to spy on the Duchess, he has a mistress, Julia, wife to Castruchio (not a chance name), and once she knows too much he has her killed, as he similarly planned for Bosola to be killed once he had served the brothers' purposes. The manner of Julia's death is particularly cruel too, as the Cardinal has poisoned the Bible she kisses.[4] There is no mistaking the irony of Ferdinand's saying to his sister: "You live in a rank pasture here, i'the court." Bosola's comment that "And though continually we bear about us/A rotten and dead body, we delight/To hide it in rich tissue" seems most pertinent too.

There is a consistency about the Duchess, Antonio, Ferdinand and the Cardinal, though: it would not be wrong to call them one-dimensional. Bosola is different. Initially he is a crook, a spy who is trusted by the Duchess and Antonio and betrays their plans to the brothers. Despite his early words "What creature ever fed worse than hoping Tantalus", he nonetheless hopes for preferment by working for the brothers. His disillusionment begins when, initially having arranged the murder of the Duchess, he is threatened by Ferdinand with death, and refused the expected pension. No gratitude. That's when he realises that it was wrong to be a true servant rather than an honest man and that he is "angry with myself, now that I wake." He then is cheered by the possibility of life still in the Duchess, and is able to assure her, as she dies, that Antonio is till living. He goes to Milan, despondent, where he hears that the Cardinal has fallen out of favour, flirts with Julia, and then is promised a fortune by the Cardinal to kill Antonio. But he has changed. No longer is he a servant of a ruthless master; now he plans to seek out Antonio, warn him and help him both escape **and** revenge. Mistakenly, though, he kills Antonio, but then stabs both the Cardinal and Ferdinand to death. He claims that he had acted previously "'gainst mine own good nature" and is penitent. He dies from a wound inflicted in an earlier scuffle with Ferdinand, but we have witnessed the progress of a journeyman spy to a man with a conscience, eventually siding with love and justice. He is by far the most interesting character in *The Duchess of Malfi*.

Not only is Bosola interesting but Webster also gives him some of the best lines. His comment on the precarious nature of life in the court is:

> "…I must look to my footing;
> In such slippery ice-pavements men had need
> To be frost-nailed well: they may break their necks else."

He comments on the law to the Cardinal:

> "When thou kill'd'st thy sister,
> Thou took'st from Justice her most equal balance
> And left her naught but her sword."

Lines that linger, but also create the mood and values of the corrupt society that Webster is depicting. Basically power enables the wielders thereof to make the law. In Act 1 Scene 2 of the play Antonio has labelled Ferdinand as being of "a most perverse and turbulent nature", and Delio adds that

> "…the law to him
> Is like a foul black cobweb to a spider,
> He makes it his dwelling, and a prison
> To entangle those shall feed him."

Ferdinand too at the end of the play is receiving medical treatment for lycanthropia: believing himself to be a wolf, he digs up dead bodies from churchyards at night. No one needs **him** as a brother!

What we witness in *The Duchess of Malfi* are corrupt courtiers and churchmen abusing their positions by enacting a kind of merciless revenge on those who will not conform to their dictates, and getting rid of others, Julia and Bosola, when they have served their purposes. It is a totally unpleasant world, but it is a world that Webster creates with excitement and energy, not only in the plot but also in the intensity of his metaphors and verse. I have quoted a good deal deliberately, and hope that the quality of his verse has at least partially been conveyed.

I want to leave the last words on *The Duchess of Malfi* with Bosola. Acceptance of Fate as opposed to a personally generated freedom are perennial issues in tragedy. Increasingly it would seem as we see the development of tragedy, it is character that determines the fate of the protagonists. In this play, though, Antonio accepts his fate, and more memorably Bosola says:

> "We are the stars' tennis balls, struck and banded
> Which way please them."

The issue of fate and freedom is one that will never be resolved, but in a rampantly capitalist world where the rich get richer and the poor get poorer the lack of control that most people have over their lives is frightening. Even when Bosola attempts to play the system there are no rewards.

It is time to look at *'Tis Pity She's a Whore*. It is customary to think of the Renaissance theatre as being heavily populated with revenge plays, but the two I have chosen do not fit entirely comfortably into that category. In both plays it is disobedience and not accepting societies' norms that are being punished by, on the one hand brothers, and on the other a husband. The story of *'Tis Pity She's a Whore* is again one of two lovers, Giovanni and Annabella, only in this play they are brother and sister. It is a mutually enjoyed affair, but, for obvious reasons, kept under wraps. Suitors acceptable to her father Florio pay courtship to Annabella; she is completely uninterested, but eventually selects Soranzo. However, she is pregnant – by her brother – and the friar, who has been advising Giovanni, thinks it politic that she marries Soranzo before the pregnancy is obvious. After the elaborate marriage ceremony Soranzo discovers that his new wife is pregnant. Soranzo vows, and plots, vengeance, against his cheating wife and her so far unknown lover. Deviously – of course! – he discovers that her brother Giovanni is the father of the child in Annabella's womb. Annabella warns her brother of Soranzo's knowledge of their love and its consequences, writing him a letter in blood. Giovanni, with a deal of arrogance, ignores the letter and attends Soranzo's birthday party. On his way to the party, however, Giovanni visits his sister, stabs her to death while kissing her, takes her heart on a dagger to the party, and admits the incest. Pandemonium! Florio dies from shock, Soranzo and Giovanni are both stabbed and die. The Church seizes everybody's wealth.

There is a subplot, revolving Hippolita, a previous lover of Soranzo, Soranzo and his servant Vasques. Hippolita had thought that Soranzo had engineered the forthcoming death of her husband so that he could marry her. But then Soranzo abandons her. She wants revenge, and colludes with Vasques, he promising to marry Hippolita once they have murdered Soranzo. During the masque at the wedding of Soranzo and Annabella Hippolita reveals herself, drinks a toast with Soranzo, believing that his glass has been poisoned. Vasques, though, has been a loyal servant and revealed all to his master and he has poisoned Hippolita. Hippolita dies, hurling vicious prophecies at the newly married couple. Vasques then worms his way into the confidence of Putana, Annabella's tutoress, and thereby discovers that Giovanni is the father of the child. Vasques then sees to it that Putana has her eyes put out. At the end of the play, as well as the Cardinal appropriating everyone's money, he orders Putana to be burned at the stake and Vasques to be banished. It is the Cardinal who utters the final words: "Who could not say, 'tis pity she's a whore."

(There is a further subplot too involving Hippolita's husband and his niece, but I think it not too relevant here and indeed it is often omitted when the play is staged.)

I hope the outline I have given is proof enough of the deceitful, corrupt court, almost glorifying in cruelty. Revenge is claimed to be the justification for such unpleasantness, though the blinding and burning at the stake of Putana seems excessively over the top. Otherwise revenge clearly motivates the actions, both of Hippolita and Soranzo: "Revenge shall sweeten what my griefs have tasted" avers Hippolita, and Soranzo delays his vengeance to deal "a heavier blow", commenting that "Revenge is all the ambition I aspire."

'Tis Pity She's a Whore ticks the box of being a revenge play. It also ticks the box of being a love play. There is not a shade of doubt about the mutual attraction of Giovanni and Annabella, but they are brother and sister. Despite what Florio their father initially says:

"I will not force my daughter 'gainst her will...
...I would not have her marry wealth but love"

this progressive thinking does not include incest. Giovanni's confidant, the friar, has also advised him to repent and forget about Annabella. "Must I not do what all men else may, love?" asks Giovanni, and the answer, in any society, is that if love involves incest it is forbidden: indeed embedded in the British nation's consciousness is the anonymous (often misattributed to Oscar Wilde "you should try everything once except incest and Morris dancing.") I suppose the acceptance of incest does sound like opening the floodgates to profligate immorality. It was certainly de trop for the citizens of Parma in the sixteenth century. But did it warrant the excesses of condemnation and brutal revenge that Ford portrays? Even though he has advised Giovanni against his love for his sister, the friar flees Parma, fearing for his life, when the truth of the relationship is revealed.

And it **is** a relationship of love, unlike the betrayal and scheming and lust Ford shows all around them, and Ford does not condemn the relationship. The friar does say to Giovanni that "th'art too far sold to hell", and clearly Giovanni has character flaws, such as arrogance, but the audience is always on the side of the lovers. Maybe it is this failure of condemnation that has led to *'Tis Pity She's a Whore* being infrequently, until recently, played, and there have also been prudish attempts to change its name to something more euphemistic. The collected edition of Ford's plays in 1831 omitted the play altogether! Declan Donnellan, though, has produced popular versions of the play in 1980 and 2011, the latter of which, as I write, is still touring. Perhaps we are closer to accepting the possibility of incest... I have mentioned the cupidity and avarice of the Catholic Church, but just as in *The Duchess of Malfi* it is seen, through the behaviour of the Cardinal, as being corrupt and murderous: as Florio say, "there's no help in this/When cardinals think murder's not amiss." The Catholic Church was an easy and popular – and almost certainly appropriate – target and the Jacobean and Caroline playwrights scored many bullseyes.

There is also the matter of the position of women. The Duchess of Malfi, perhaps emboldened by her title **and** her experience, was a strong woman. She made the running in her relationship with Antonio. In *'Tis Pity She's a Whore* it is Giovanni who makes the running, but, although less of a feminist icon than the Duchess of Malfi, Annabella nonetheless clearly is a strong woman, pursuing her own wishes and desires, flagrantly contrary to the values of the court around her. That court and its wish to control the marriages of its women ensure that she compromises by marrying Soranzo, but there is a strength in what she does. It is not a woman's world: it is a world in which Soranzo can boast:

> "Yet will not I forget what I should be,
> And what I am, a husband; in that name
> Is hid divinity"

and confidently proclaim that frailty and woman are close synonyms.

The final point I wish to make about *'Tis Pity She's a Whore* is how it unites the question of character and free will, the eternal question as to how much control we have over our actions. We may feel we are compelled, have no choice, to behave as we do, but is this on account of some unseen pre-ordained script-written fate, and is this fate written in the stars or does it stem from who we are by nature? This play addresses that issue very clearly. The power of love is the root cause of everything in *'Tis Pity She's a Whore*. It is seen as an uncontrollable necessity by Giovanni and Annabella – and millions of novels and pop songs and personal romantic encounters attest to this. When it is mutual urge it is something wonderful – yet this is not a defence in a court of law, with regard to incest, adultery, under-age sex etc. Love is not above the law: "we loved each other" is no defence. Yet Annabella and Giovanni pass the responsibility for their lust to Fate. Annabella says to her brother:

> "Wouldst thou hadst been less subject to those stars
> That luckless reigned at my nativity."

Giovanni, though, has already explained to the Friar that "'tis not/My lust, but 'tis my fate that leads me on." And then, finally and gloriously, Giovanni takes responsibility:

> "Fate, or all the powers
> That guide the motions of immortal souls
> Could not prevent me."

We have an acknowledgment of the power of love and an acceptance of personal involvement in one's actions. In many ways *Tis Pity She's a Whore* is a modern play in so far as it offers no judgments, and in other ways it is a bloody, decadent romp, energised by cruelty and revenge. However you look at it, it stimulates.

---

[1] Both plays could be seen in the United Kingdom in the first half of 2014.

[2] But even in *Titus Andronicus* Shakespeare makes his villains far more rounded than ever Webster does. For example Aaron, indisputably a blackguard, is shown as literate and well versed in the classics.

[3] Cariola, the Duchess's woman servant thinks and voices this.

[4] This echoes a similar murder device employed by Webster in *The White Devil* when a character kisses the poisoned portrait of the man she loves.

JOHN MILTON: *Samson Agonistes*

First thoughts might well question why I have included *Samson Agonistes* in this book on tragedy in so far as Milton never intended it to be performed on stage[1]: it was simply a "dramatic poem", deliberately following the rules for tragedy laid down by Aristotle. And, without, wishing to become too academic about Aristotle's edicts, that is why I have included this chapter on *Samson Agonistes* – also I have included three other chapters on dramas that are tragedies of the highest order but are not theatre pieces.

Samson Agonistes was published in the same volume as 'Paradise Regained' in 1671, eleven years after the restoration of the monarchy with Charles II and the failure of the republican revolution. There is some doubt as to when exactly Samson Agonistes was written, for Samson was a figure that clearly fascinated Milton, as there are numerous references to him as a subject for tragedy in his 1640's notebooks. The truth is that we just don't know when it was written, so it's best to let speculation go, as, I believe, is too much concentration on the parallels between Milton's blindness and that of Samson. Yes, Milton knew something about blindness, but he is not equating his travails with those of Samson.

The story is simple enough. Samson is "eyeless in Gaza", using his still enormous strength to do building work for his Philistine enemies. He is fed for his labours, but, being blind, can do nothing but submit to his captors' wishes. He is visited in turn by the Chorus of sympathetic Israelites, his father Manoa, his wife Dalila and Harapa of Gath, an enemy giant. Manoa is trying to arrange the ransom of his son, Dalila is seeking some kind of reconciliation and Harapa is taunting Samson that his strength lies only in his hair. In the course of the dialogue between these people we are told the back story of Samson, of his terrific feats of strength, such as defeating enemies with "an ass's jaw." We are told too of his strength being given him by God, with the instruction that he should not disclose to anyone the secret of where his strength comes from. Enter Dalila (and we are not thinking Tom Jones here!), the Philistine femme fatale, whom Samson falls in love with, to whom he reveals God's secrets. She cuts his hair, betrays him to the Philistines who capture him and blind him. Samson knows he deserves to be punished for breaking his pact with God, so is reluctant to be ransomed, refuses point blank to have anything further to do with Dalila and pitifully challenges the mocking Harapa to fight. Another visitor enters: it is a Public Officer, bidding Samson attend the feast of Dagon, the Philistine god and there to entertain the assembled crowd with his feats of strength. Initially Samson refuses, on the grounds that he will not condescend to participate in the worship of any other god than that of Israel. However when the Public Officer comes again, threatening to make Samson attend by the use of force, Samson acquiesces, takes his leave and accompanies him. Then, while his father Manoa is talking of maybe succeeding in ransoming Samson, a hideous noise is heard off stage, "a universal groan" containing "blood, death and deathful deeds." Soon a messenger appears with the full story: Samson has entertained the Philistines, and then asked, because he is tired, to be stood between the pillars of the spacious theatre so the pillars could support him. Whereupon he tugged at the pillars of the theatre until he brought down the pillars and the whole roof, killing the "choice nobility and flower, not only/Of this but each Philistian City around." Samson too is dead, of course, but gloriously so.

The Aristotle connection is spelt out by Milton in his Preface to *Samson Agonistes*. It goes almost without saying that the decline of Samson, from strength to weakness, is of the stuff of the tragic hero. But in the Preface Milton specifically alludes to introducing the Chorus "after the Greek manner" and referring to Aristotle's belief that tragedy raises pity and fear, or terror, in order to purge the mind of such passions. Milton wanted none of the mixing of "Comic stuff with Tragic sadness and gravity" or introducing "trivial and vulgar persons." He was following the Greek model, seeing Tragedy as "the gravest, moralist, and most profitable" art form. Milton wants *Samson Agonistes* to be judged by those who are well acquainted with Aeschylus, Sophocles and Euripides. You probably noticed that in the story line I outlined the staged action took place was in one place only and, by the Greek device of the

Chorus to fill in the past, it took place in real time, i.e. it conformed to what Aristotle called the Unities of space and time. The last words too of *Samson Agonistes* are "calm of mind all passion spent", indicating that a full catharsis, a purging of the emotions, has taken place, as Aristotle promoted.

So as an English template of an ideal Greek tragedy *Samson Agonistes* is memorable. But there is so much more to it than that. For one thing there is the interesting blend of Greek format with Hebrew history. Clearly by the time of the action of *Samson Agonistes* the Philistines were the enemy of Israel, but this had not always been so. They ruled the five city states of Gaza, Ashkelon, Ashdod, Ekron and Gath, but they are not amongst the ten tribes mentioned in Genesis when the Lord's covenant with Abraham promises him and his descendants the land "from the river of Egypt unto the great river, the river Euphrates." Indeed in Genesis Chapter 21 Abraham makes a covenant at Beer-sheba with the Philistine leader Abimelech and sojourns "many days" in the land of the Philistines. And when Moses, in Deuteronomy, tells of the nations that Israel should take and possess there is no mention of the Philistines. In the Torah too there is no mention of the Philistines having to be displaced from Canaan. Their reputation, though, is warlike. The Samson story does not end the conflict between Israel and the Philistines – it is left to David, with his sling and a stone, to kill Goliath and complete the process. Samson, though, along with David, is the great hero of Israel in the defeat of the Philistines.

The Samson story is taken from Judges Chapter 13 to 16 – and unlike Shakespeare Milton takes no liberties with his subject. The dramatic format, though, the dialogues between Samson and his visitors, is all crafted by Milton. There is no doubt of the heroic capacity of Samson. An angel twice visited his previously barren parents, assuring them that their child Samson was "designed for great exploits" and "should Israel from Philistian yoke deliver." Samson should be brought up as a Nazarite, which meant that he should drink nothing that came from the grape and therefore absolutely no alcohol, that he should never cut his hair and that he should have no contact with corpses or graves. (Unfortunately there were no restrictions placed on sexualising with women.) All went according to plan and Samson committed great feats of strength, acknowledged by the taunting strongman rival Harapah:

> "Much have I heard
> Of thy prodigious might and feats performed
> Incredible to me."

Along the way Philistines had been killed too – "with a trivial weapon (I) felled their choicest youth." All was on course for his final vanquishing of the Philistines. Then along came Dalila. And the great man, through a common human failing, is brought down, blinded, imprisoned and is made a helpless captive of the people he was supposed to defeat. Samson has followed the path, from greatness to failure, of the tragic hero. "Strongest of mortal men,/To lowest pitch of abject fortune art thou fallen" comments the Chorus. But all is not lost! As he bids farewell to the Chorus he expresses the hope that "This day will be remarkable in my life/By some great act, or of my days the last." He duly brings down the theatre and the assembled mighty amongst the Philistines ("the vulgar only escaped") and, in death, attains the glory of his former stature: "Samson hath quit himself like Samson," says his father.

Milton has kept very faithfully to the Bible story. What he has added, though, are the insights into the workings of Samson's mind. The initial indication of this is in the title of the play – *Samson* **Agonistes**. Agonistes means struggling, deriving from participating in public games. In Milton's play Samson is struggling with himself, and agonising over his plight. Samson is fully aware of his own shortcomings and how his default on the agreement with God not to tell anyone wherein lay his strength has scuppered God's purpose for him. As he laments: "what is strength without a double share of wisdom?" Dalila made him traitor to himself and he fully accepts he deserves his situation – for him he is in the dark, without all hope of light, within the dungeon of himself and there is no light for his soul.[2] He has brought it all upon himself: "foul effeminacy had me yoked", and in his mind he deserves to be "sung and proverbed for a Fool in every street." He beats himself up with having brought scandal to Israel and pomp and honour to the infidel Philistine god, Dagon. Samson does not want his father to rescue him by ransom: he fully merits his staying in Philistine hands and receiving his punishment. It is all "mea culpa." The Chorus advocates Patience, but Samson sees himself drudging and earning Philistine bread, until death. Indeed he welcomes death. Sleep eludes him and he sees "death's benumming Opium" as his "only cure." This genuine brow-beating is in the first part of the play, before the different dialogues gather pace. There is no indication that Samson has any plans to triumph over the disaster he has created. It is all introspection and self-blame, misery and darkness, contrasting splendidly with his glorious final triumph. This agonising, this struggling with what his weakness has brought about is, together with the verse, the most important thing that Milton has brought to the Bible story, and is in the English tragic tradition too – of Shakespeare's Hamlet and Othello et al.

Both Manoa and Harapha are one-dimensional characters. The only other slightly complex person in *Samson Agonistes* is Dalila. Samson fell in love with this woman from the valley of Sorek, and she, at the fourth time of asking, at the behest of the Philistines, "with feminine assaults, tongue-batteries … in her highth of Nuptial Love" wrested from Samson the secret that his strength lay in his hair and betrayed him to the Philistines. It would be easy to label her a one-dimensional villain and leave it at that. But Milton makes her so much more interesting. In the first place he has it that she and Samson were married, which was not so in the Bible. In his railing Samson calls her "a deceitful Concubine", but their marriage is attested to by his disapproving father – and indeed by Dalila and by the Chorus

Wife or mistress is, arguably, a minor distinction. The most interesting thing that Milton does is to bring Dalila before the shorn Samson for them to engage in the most dramatic dialogue of the whole play or "dramatic poem." She is seen arriving "bedeckt, ornate and gay …sailing like a stately Ship of Tarsus …with all her bravery on and tackle trim, sails filled and streamers waving." She explains how full of fear she was to see Samson again, but her "conjugal affection" was stronger than her fear, and she is now desirous to serve him somehow "in some part to recompense/My rash but more unfortunate deed." She knows she was wrong to reveal Samson's secret to his enemies, but she spells out a plausible explanation for her behaviour: in the first place the Philistines had promised that no harm would come to Samson once deprived of his hair and strength and then she spells out her foremost reasoning. She loved Samson so much and wanted to enjoy him "day and night … in bed", but she knew that his strength and freedom would mean that he would be taken away from her "to perilous enterprises." What she had in mind was that Samson should be "Mine and Love's prisoner, not the Philistines." What she did, she did for love. Samson will have none of it; he calls her a hyaena, insists she sold him to the Philistines for gold and that what she calls Love is merely Lust. He is totally contemptuous of her.

Dalila also advances the argument that she was approached by Magistrates and Princes of her country to do her duty by her religion and her nation – thus sacrificing Samson was for the public good, which was more important than her private pleasure. Samson simply sees the marriage vow as stronger than all other commitments. Then Dalila makes one final attempt to make recompense for her betrayal by offering to take him from the prison and to nurse and tend him into old age with her "redoubled love." Samson is appalled at this suggestion, and when Dalila approaches and asks at least to touch his hand, he explodes. Finally she gets the message as to how full of rage and hatred Samson is towards her, and she departs, boasting that however defamed she might be amongst the circumcised Israelites, she would be named "amongst the famousest of women" in the history of the Philistine nation.

It is the "wedlock treachery" that Samson cannot forgive. When she departs, Dalila leaves Samson to his lot and says how she likes her own lot. It is a fascinating dialogue. In many ways what Dalila says is plausible. But is there a subtext or an ulterior purpose to her meeting with Samson? When she claims superiority as she leaves, is this an attempt to save a little pride and dignity or has there all along been something malicious behind her attempts to regain Samson's affections. I tend to take her at face value and believe that she is penitent and means well, but readily concede that there is an alternative interpretation. I find this version of her – Milton's version – fascinating, as, I guess, Samson at one time did!

It is good to see a strong female character – like Cleopatra or Rosalind – at the heart of *Samson Agonistes*. But, whereas Shakespeare puts words into the mouth of Hamlet such as "frailty thy name is woman", that is a character's personal response to a particular predicament and there is no suggestion of misogyny in Shakespeare's view of the world, with Milton this cannot be said to be true. Samson's railing against Dalila is entirely understandable considering her extreme betrayal, but – just possibly on account of Milton's personal experience – there is a strong degree of believing in the inferiority of women in *Samson Agonistes*. I am not talking about the conciliatory responses of the Chorus to Samson that "wisest Men have erred, and by bad women been deceived." What I am referring to is that both the Chorus **and** Dalila concur that "the specious monster (and) deceitful concubine" Dalila's behaviour in shoring Samson "like a tame Weather" is not untypical of women in general.

Dalila herself talks of women's frailty and weakness and links them with curiosity and the inability to keep a secret:
"Curiosity, inquisitive, importune
Of secrets, then with like infirmity
To publish them, both common female faults" she concedes. She also believes that whatever the subject women will always lose in an argument with men. A distinctly debatable proposition, but accepted by all in *Samson Agonistes*.

It is the Chorus, though, which confirms the underlying misogyny of the play. The long speech from line 1100 onwards demonstrates this. The Chorus talks of "outward ornament" being lavished "on their Sex" at the expense of judgment. Women's self-love means that either they are incapable of any love or of sustaining love. Each woman – apparently – :
"Seeming at first all heavenly under a virgin veil,
Soft, modest, meek, demure,
Once joined, the contrary she proves, a thorn…"

But not quite all women: rarely one finds a virtuous woman "favoured of Heaven". Such a one makes a happy, domestic home for the man. The Chorus concludes from this that:
"Therefore God's universal Law
Gave to the man despotic power
Over his female in due awe."

By any modern standards Milton's view of women is unhealthy.

That mention of God in the above quotation is a reminder that the Old Testament God of the Jews is everywhere in *Samson Agonistes*. The Jews have no doubt that their God is the only good God and that they are the chosen people, and so the story told – just as the New Testament is basically propaganda for the Christian religion – is similarly propaganda for the Jewish religion. Milton recreates very well the Jewish mindset that sees "Just are the ways of God/And justifiable to men", and scorn is poured upon "the heart of the Fool" who thinks there is no God. God is not bound by the laws he has laid down for men. When his father suggests that God has gone too far in permitting Samson to be so drastically punished, Samson will have none of it: he alone is responsible: "I myself have brought them on, Sole Author," though he now feels cast off by God "as never known." But there is no doubt about the strength and purpose of God. Samson knows that he will "arise and his great name assert" over the heathen's God Dagon, and Manoa thinks that nothing is more certain than that God "will not long defer/To vindicate the glory of his name/Against all competition." And Samson is, of course, his agent that accomplishes this: he has served God's ultimate purpose prescribed at birth and justified his "trust in the living God who gave me/At my nativity this strength."

This dramatic poem *Samson Agonistes* is this fascinating mixture of Greek dramaturgy and Jewish religion. Milton has accepted the Hebrew belief about Samson and his vocation given him by God at birth[3] – but I think there is an English protestant sensibility to be found in *Samson Agonistes* too, almost an acceptance of some form of predetermination or predestination. Samson's anger is directed pretty much at himself; he is not a Christ figure lamenting that his God has forsaken him. Nearly half way through *Samson Agonistes* the Chorus, with apparent resignation, asserts:

> "Just or unjust, alike seem miserable,
> For oft alike, both come to evil end."

And the opening words of its final speech are:

> "All is best, though we oft doubt,
> What the unsearchable dispose
> Of highest Wisdom brings about."

Basically the overriding perspective on things is that *it's all in the hands of the gods*. That owes a deal to Greek drama, though in Greek drama the gods can at least be approached and negotiated with. If we say *it's all in the hands of God* then we have much more a Calvinist viewpoint. I don't want to overstress the Englishness of this play, though I find Manoa's eminently reasonable argument that:

"Repent the sin, but if the punishment
Thou canst avoid, self-preservation bids"

very pragmatically English! The fundamental point is, though, that however we look at it, *Samson Agonistes* is a drama of quality that warrants study.

---

1. Milton calls *Samson Agonistes* "a dramatic poem."

2. There is a splendid description of blindness in Sean O'Casey's play *The Silver Tassie* when Teddy, blinded in the First World War, says that his "darkness stretches from the throne of God to the deep heart of Hell."

3. Obviously a religion to strengthen its appeal will use apparently supernatural visitations as propaganda. How much of this is added in hindsight and how much genuinely believed at the time of the experience we will never know. But people who believe they are on a divine mission, such as Tony Blair, and people who do things because they are certain that they are right, such as Ian Duncan Smith, fill me with dread.

VERDI: *Rigoletto*

When one considers the origins of Opera it makes sense to me to include a chapter about an opera. I have chosen *Rigoletto* partly because it is my favourite opera and partly because it fulfils many of the criteria of tragedy. Opera had its beginnings with a group of Florentine poets and musicians, the Camerata, meeting in the last twenty years of the sixteenth century, that was fascinated by Greek tragedy and its use of poetry and music to create drama. Aristotle's *Poetics* was their bible, proclaiming that language in tragedy "has the embellishments of rhythm melody and metre... In some parts metre alone is employed, in others, melody." Tragedy – with music – was a high art form to which to aspire, and from 1607 onwards, with the performance of Monteverdi's *Orfeo*, Opera became a very serious art form with wonderful contributions to the genre from Purcell, Handel, Mozart, Beethoven, Berlioz, Rossini, Donizetti, Verdi, Wagner, Bizet, Chabrier, Tchaikovsky, Puccini, Charpentier, Richard Strauss, Berg, Janacek, Britten and Glass – to mention but a few.

So the fact that there are very few happy endings in Opera is entirely due to the nature of the genre. Whether it is students or courtesans dying of consumption, singers jumping off battlements, Japanese women committing suicide, cigarette workers being stabbed to death on the day of a bullfight or daughters being stabbed to death and thus fulfilling a dying father's curse, the world of Opera is awash with tragic finales. There are links too with tragedies we have already looked at: Handel's oratorio *Samson* (though sometimes presented as an opera) was first performed in 1784 and owed a good deal to Milton; Saint-Saens explored the same subject in *Samson et Dalila* in 1877. More pertinently we think of Verdi having written *Macbeth* and *Otello*, the latter sticking especially close to Shakespeare's play. (Of course Verdi also wrote *Falstaff* – as did Salieri – which is a very light-hearted opera, and is an example of not all operas being tragic **and** an example of the range of skills of the genius that was Verdi.)

The origins of Opera, though, were in Greek tragedy. Thinking for a moment of the modern musical we can still trace the debt owed to tragedy in the fates of Porgy, Billy Bigelow, Tony and Maria and (almost) Gaylord Ravenal, but the thrust in modern musicals is towards a happy ending.

And, of course, someone like Billy Bigelow has little stature in the community. The days have long gone when only kings or mythical heroes could be the subject of tragedy – a significant lapse or fall or indeed a horrendous final confrontation suffices. So it is with Rigoletto in Verdi's opera of that name. We know little of the past of Rigoletto, either in Verdi's opera or in Victor Hugo's *Le Roi S'Amuse*, the play from which Verdi and his librettist Francesco Maria Piave took their source. Writing to Piave, Verdi hailed the Hugo play as "the best plot and perhaps the best play of modern times." But just as Hugo's play was banned after one performance and not seen on the French stage for another fifty years, so Venice's Department of Public Order rejected *Rigoletto* for its "disgusting immorality and obscene triviality of the plot." The French censors of Hugo's play thought there were parallels between the French king having fun in the play and the current king on the throne, and the Italian censorship was also unhappy about its depiction of royalty. But all Piave and Verdi had to do for *Rigoletto* to be accepted was for Francois I in the original text to be changed to the apolitical Duke of Mantua and all was well – reservations about the immortality and obscenity, or the sex/lechery and violence, seemingly vanishing. First performed on March 11th 1851 *Rigoletto* was an instant both dramatic and musical success. In the ten years after its opening night it was performed nearly three hundred times and remains a much loved staple in any operatic company's repertoire.

So much for the background. This is the story. As I said, we know little about Rigoletto, and therefore his daughter Gilda's, background, except that once he was in a loftier position somewhere. Now he is the hunchbacked court jester to the Duke of Mantua. The Duke is a lecherous libertine, bent on seducing any attractive woman, with the full leering complicity of his all male court, including Rigoletto. When Rigoletto mocks Count Ceprano whose wife is being seduced by the Duke, the courtiers suggest that the Count could revenge himself by seducing Rigoletto's mistress (in fact the occasionally glimpsed woman living with Rigoletto is his daughter Gilda). Nothing comes of this suggestion but a seed has been sown. When another Count, Monterone, rails at the Duke for seducing his daughter and is duly arrested, Rigoletto again joins in the mockery and the Count places a curse on Rigoletto.

At home – after a fortuitous and eventually fortunate(?) encounter with an assassin touting for business – Rigoletto, knowing full well the zeitgeist of Mantua, pleads with his attractive daughter never to leave the house unaccompanied. Unknown to her father, though, Gilda has met a young man at church and fallen in love with him, not knowing that this young man was the Duke in disguise. She confesses this to her nurse Giovanna, but is overheard by the Duke, who, pretending to be a poor student, shares a confession of mutual love with Gilda. On Rigoletto's return the courtiers involve by trickery Rigoletto's complicity in the abduction of Gilda. Once he realises that it is his own daughter that has been kidnapped Rigoletto collapses and remembers the curse that had been placed upon him.

That is Act 1. In Act 2 Rigoletto confronts and condemns the courtiers for their action. In keeping with the mood of the Court they mock him. But when the somewhat distressed and ashamed Gilda appears, having been rescued and (it is assumed) seduced by the Duke, she pleads on behalf of the Duke, whereas Rigoletto is bent on revenge.

This incompatibility of their feelings towards the Duke has to be resolved in the third Act. But it never is, as Gilda remains loving to the end and Rigoletto is bent on his murder. To this latter end Rigoletto has engaged Sparafucile, the assassin he had previously encountered. Sparafucile runs an inn on the outskirts of Mantua, where the Duke is a visitor and is seen and heard, by Gilda and Rigoletto, attempting to seduce Sparafucile's sister Maddalena. Once the murder (price 20 scudi) has been committed, Rigoletto intends to flee with Gilda to Verona. For this purpose Gilda dresses as a man but returns to the inn. She overhears Maddalena, having fallen, like so many women, for the Duke, pleading to spare the Duke's life, and her brother saying that if another male knocks on the door before midnight then that person will take the Duke's place as the murder victim. Gilda knocks on the door and is stabbed – the Duke's life is spared and she has sacrificed herself for love. Rigoletto then arrives with the payment but before he throws the corpse in a sack into the river he hears the Duke singing. He rips open the sack and discovers his beloved daughter on her deathbed. She asserts that she is nonetheless glad that she has died for the man she loved but also begs her father's forgiveness for deceiving him. Gilda dies in Rigoletto's arms and he is left in total agony believing that Monterone's curse has been fulfilled.

Rigoletto is a controversial tragic hero. He does dominate the stage, but he is unattractive: there is not only his physical deformity[1] but he is morally reprehensible, taking a sneering delight in members of the court being cuckolded by the Duke. In many ways he can be seen as an outsider, desperately conforming to the morals of the Mantuan court in a failed attempt to fit in and be accepted. Perhaps this very insecurity leads to what is in fact a pretty reprehensible schadenfreude. Chances are he is a nobleman fallen on hard times, but we hear little of that, so he cannot be said to have fallen from a position of some significance. Rigoletto's most praiseworthy quality is his unqualified devotion to his daughter (though he tries to run a very controlling and repressive regime); his concern for her after her abduction is heartfelt and then for her to die in his arms after a murder that he himself had instigated and financed is truly heartbreaking. It is something with which all fathers can identify – and certainly arouses pity and fear.

We, the audience, can readily see what is Rigoletto's fatal weakness: he has double standards, one for womankind in general and another for his own daughter. The first are always fair game, while the second has to be protected against the fate he exults in when it befalls other women. There is no realisation of this contradictory thinking by Rigoletto: there is agony, but without the intelligent soul-searching we have in Shakespeare's tragedies. In fact Rigoletto blames everything on fate, specifically the curse laid on him by Count Monterone at the outset. The whole concept of fate runs through tragedy from the Greeks onwards – the House of Atreus had to work through its curse. Hamlet laments what he saw as the curse of his responsibility; "The time is out of joint. O cursed spite/That ever I was born to set it right." Rigoletto uses the concept of the curse/fate to wriggle out of his personal responsibility.²

In reality, by the deflowering and killing (both of reputation and body) of Gilda, a kind of rough justice is meted out to Rigoletto: his daughter meets the fate he has been advocating for other women. He fails to see the connection. The opera *Rigoletto*, though, with its questioning of personal responsibility, its creation of a climate which presents moral dilemmas, its need for the puncturing of hubris, its dramatic use of the concept of fate and its final evocation of pity and fear ranges through territory which can truly be called tragic.

It is the pity and fear which ultimately remain. Verdi himself had suffered the loss of his children and his first wife in successive years from 1838 to 1840: his daughter Virginia died in 1838 aged 16 months, his son Ilito died in the following year aged 15 months, and then his wife of four years, Margharita, died of encephalitis aged 26 in 1840. Verdi had reason to empathise with Rigoletto's lot. It was eleven years later, however, that *Rigoletto* triumphed, followed by the other two great operas of his middle period, *Il Trovatore* and *La Traviata*. Seven years after the death of Margharita Verdi began, somewhat scandalously, to co-habit with La Scala's soprano Giuseppina Strepponi; they married in 1859 and remained together until her death in 1897 – she had been influential in La Scala accepting Verdi's unsolicited opera *Oberto* in 1839 and she was the first Abigaille in his *Nabucco* (1842).

Inevitably, because of the whole thesis of this book, I have been considering *Rigoletto* as a stage drama, perhaps criminally without reference to the music! It is Verdi's music rather than Victor Hugo's original play and Piave's libretto which makes *Rigoletto* such a wonderful opera. The first thing that strikes the listener is the proliferation of wonderful tunes: the obvious ones are the Duke's introductory aria *"Questo o quella"*, Gilda's heart-stopping *"Caro nome"*, the stunning beauty of the quartet *"Bella figlia dell'amore"* (surely no quartet can surpass this) and, of course, *"La donna e mobile."* With this latter aria Verdi knew he had a hit on his hands, so the cast were forbidden to sing or hum it outside the rehearsal room, and sure enough, after the first performance, the tune was on everyone's lips. But, in the context of tragedy, it more significantly played a major part: it is the Duke's signature, and just before Rigoletto is to throw the sack into the river he hears the Duke singing *"La donna e mobile"* – he is alive! So whose is the body in the sack? A truly electrifying moment.

It is wrong, though, to see *Rigoletto* merely through its tunes. Musicologists, such as Julian Budden[3], tell me that it is revolutionary. There is no overture, only a suggestive fate-filled prelude; the chorus is all male; there are no ensemble finales at the end of each Act; the action does not stop for any self-identifying arias. The drama, the interaction between the characters on stage is paramount. Verdi wrote that "I conceived *Rigoletto* almost without arias, without finales but only an unending string of duets." In reality it is not all duets, but this kind of thinking was new and the conventional form of the nineteenth century opera was dead.

I hope I have made a sufficient case for this chapter on Verdi, and on *Rigoletto* in particular, but I want to conclude by quoting Isiah Berlin and thereby resting my case: "Noble, simple, with a degree of unbroken vitality and vast natural power of creation and organisation, Verdi is the voice of a world that is no more. His enormous popularity among the sophisticated as well as the most ordinary listeners today is due to the fact that he expressed permanent states of consciousness in the most direct terms, as Homer, Shakespeare, Ibsen and Tolstoy have done."

* * *

I have written about Rigoletto, a man "inwardly passionate and full of love" as Verdi described him, as my example of a tragic hero. But it is noteworthy how many tragic heroines there are in some of the most popular operas: there is Violetta, the courtesan who dies of consumption in Verdi's wonderful *La Traviata*; there is Salome in Richard Strauss's opera of the same name; there is Berg's *Lulu*. Femmes fatales all. And Strauss went to Sophocles' *Electra* for another female-centred opera.

All these operas are frequently performed. But the composer who has the tragic death of a woman in so many of his operas is Puccini. Puccini was an avaricious devourer of women in his personal life and some critics have added misogyny to sickly sentimentality and feeble plots and shallowness[4] to the list of negative criticism levelled at his music. But, at the very least, he knew how to write a good tune! He claimed never to have found love in his real world, but in the world of his operas he creates not only beauty, which he regarded as being the essence of high quality, but also some great love scenes and some great female characters who, of course, die for love. From his first successful opera *Manon Lescaut* to Mimi in *La Boheme* to Tosca in the opera of the same name to *Madama Butterfly* we have a succession of women for whom love has been wonderful (though in Butterfly's case delusional) but all of whom die tragically. Admittedly in *Madama Butterfly* we have a quiescent heroine, with none of the strength of Manon Lescaut or Tosca, but the music! Especially the fifteen-minute love duet between Butterfly and Pinkerton at the end of Act 1, only surpassed by the near forty-five minutes of the orgasmic love duet between Tristan and Isolde in the second Act of Wagner's musical masterpiece. Passion and death. That is what tragic opera is all about and Puccini knew how to tug at our elemental emotional chords.

---

[1] Characters with physical deformities need not be unattractive. Witness the lawyer, Shardlake in C.J.Sansom's masterly series of Tudor novels.

[2] Significantly the original and working title of *Rigoletto* was *La Maledizione* – the **Curse!**

[3] In *The Operas of Verdi, Volume 1* (1984).

[4] Benjamin Britten spoke of being "sickened by the cheapness and emptiness" of *Tosca*.

THOMAS HARDY:
The Mayor of Casterbridge

Most intelligent people read novels, and most intelligent people have their favourites. So when I choose Thomas Hardy as the one novelist that I am going to discuss I am fully aware that there will be disagreements. There will also be disagreements about the novel I have chosen: I suspect that *Tess of the d'Urbervilles* or *Jude the Obscure* or even *Far From the Madding Crowd* would have been a more popular choice, and, although I do also love those three novels, *The Mayor of Casterbridge* is, I think, the best example of the tragic form in all of Hardy's novels. And I certainly could not discuss the trials and tribulations of Bathsheba Everdene in *Far From the Madding Crowd* – for goodness sake, it has a happy ending!

I have a sense too that once lip-service has been given to the skill and craft of Jane Austen, to the Brontes *Wuthering Heights* and *Jane Eyre*, to *Middlemarch* as the best – and, according to Virginia Woolf, – the most intelligent English novel, and to Dickens for his social comment and humour, that lip-service being over, there would be a majority of modern readers favouring[1] Hardy as the most accessible and most demanding of serious attention of nineteenth century novelists.

Be all that as it may or may not be, I think I can show what a splendid example of a tragic novel is *The Mayor of Casterbridge*. Hardy classified his novels and short stories into three groups: Novels of Character and Environment[2]; Romances and Fantasies; Novels of Ingenuity. This first category is the most serious one and, of course, it is there we find *The Mayor of Casterbridge*. Written in 1886 it is then fourth of nine of these Novels of Character and Environment, following on from *Far From the Madding Crowd* (1874) and *The Return of the Native* (1878) and succeeded by *Tess of the D'Urbervilles* (1891) and *Jude the Obscure* (1896) – these five being, I believe, Hardy's most significant novels.

I shall be mainly discussing character rather than environment when I come to write about *The Mayor of Casterbridge*, but environment is very much to the fore in *The Return of the Native*. The first chapter of that novel is entitled: 'A Face on Which Time Makes but Little Impression'. It is all about the fictitious Egdon Heath, on which, often solitary characters, pass back and forth. Hardy writes: "It was at present a place perfectly accordant with man's nature – neither ghastly, hateful, nor ugly; neither commonplace, unmeaning, nor tame; but, like man, slighted and enduring; and withal singularly colossal and mysterious in its swarthy monotony. As with some persons who have long lived apart, solitude seemed to look out of its countenance. It had a lonely face, suggesting tragical possibilities." These tragical possibilities are enacted through disastrous marriages, going blind, drownings, guilt and disappointment. The fate of the characters is played out against the background of Egdon Heath and whatever their fate the Heath remains. Indeed Hardy dreams in his introduction to the 1895 edition of the novel that it "may be the heath of that traditionary King of Wessex – Lear."

Yes, environment matters to Hardy. We see this in *Tess of the D'Urbervilles* when Tess's degradation, having experienced rape, loss of a child and abandonment by her husband, is expressed by her working on the "starve-acre place" that is Flintcomb-Ash farm. Tess "slaved in the morning frosts and in the afternoon rain" grubbing for and hacking up swedes in the "desolate drab" field. "They worked on hour after hour, unconscious of the forlorn aspect they bore in the landscape, not thinking of the justice or injustice of their lot." Stonehenge too is significant at the end of the novel; it is the "heathen temple" where doubtless sacrifices took place and which is "older than the centuries; older than the d'Urbervilles." Places, landscapes survive, live on; people do not.

The main sense of place in Hardy's last novel *Jude the Obscure* is Christminster, which in reality is Oxford. The eleven-year-old Jude expresses his ambition to go there, following his former schoolmaster Phillotson at the outset of the novel, and indeed does go there, but only working as a stonemason, which he hoped would eventually finance his studies at the university. It all falls apart, however – cherchez la femme – and Jude's life ends, not yet thirty, in alcohol and poverty. Although Christminster is a city and just about on the northern boundary of Hardy's Wessex and thereby Hardy is denying himself the terrain whose mood and influence he creates so well in other novels, nonetheless both as a real location and as an aspiration it dominates *Jude the Obscure* – although it is not the city itself which destroys Jude, the boy from Marygreen in the country. Hardy presents us with a clash between flesh and spirit and it is Jude's inability to withstand the lure of the flesh which fundamentally militates against him. There are two women in Jude's life, the fleshy Arabella and his intellectual cousin Sue. We sense the power of Arabella immediately at their first meeting. To attract Jude's attention, she initially throws a pig's pizzle at him, which hit him on the ear. She then introduces herself: "My father is a pig-breeder, and these girls are helping me wash the innards for black-puddings and such like." Jude is pretty well trapped from that moment: "The unvoiced call of woman to man, which was uttered very distinctly by Arabella's personality, held Jude to the spot against his intention – almost against his will, and in a way new to his experience."

Hardy is critical of the church and unforgiving morality too in *Jude the Obscure*, but his most characteristic trait is a representation of Fate working against the plans and hopes of mere mortals. There is the best-known quotation from *Tess of the D'Urbervilles:* "'Justice' was done, and the President of the Immortals, in Aeschylean phrase, had ended his sport with Tess." In *Jude the Obscure*, as well as believing that marriage destroys love, Sue will not marry Jude because she also holds a belief that the Fawley family (Jude's – and hers) is doomed to have unhappy marriages. Indeed at one moment she likens their family to that of the house of Atreus (Aeschylus and Agamemnon et al again) and Jude talks of the fall of the idol-worshiping house of Jeroboam in Hebrew history. Hardy is very conscious of the literature and nature of history when he is writing these novels of Character and Environment.

So it can be seen that his tragic novels are very much in the mainstream of tragedy. There are so many facets to Hardy's novels and I am aware that by focusing on tragedy I am not giving a full picture of the credible world in which he so skilfully immerses the reader. But I need to move on to *The Mayor of Casterbridge*. Hardy's tragic heroes/heroines are not like Agamemnon or Samson or Jeroboam – they are not kings nor do Tess and Jude have any power in the community. We are talking of the tragedy of ordinary people. What they have in common, though, is that they have ambition or pretension: Jude wishes to study at Christminster, Tess wants to believe that she descends from an aristocratic family. Both have their pretensions pricked; both fail – in the case of Jude in the most abject way. It is not that Hardy is an establishment figure, believing that the peasants should stay in their places: far from it – Hardy's father was a stonemason whose family had seen better times, and Hardy himself, through his career as an architect and, essentially, a writer, did not keep to his born social position. And *Jude the* Obscure was denounced in the House of Lords. Indeed such was the general hostile response to the novel and its questioning the institution of marriage that Hardy subsequently, at the age of 55, foreswore writing any more novels. In his preface to the 1912 edition of *Jude the Obscure* Hardy tells of the work being "burnt by a bishop – probably in his despair at not being able to burn me."

Michael Henchard who becomes the Mayor of Casterbridge is again someone who is not born with a silver spoon in his mouth, but he does make good and it is his fall from his eminent social position that makes him such a fascinating tragic hero. As I have discussed previously tragic heroes represent archetypal human beings from whose experiences we can all learn. They are certainly not role-models! Traditionally the tragic hero has either a fatal character flaw or makes a fatal mistake, which eventually leads to some kind of nemesis or retribution and subsequent ruin. Michael Henchard's (unforgivable?) error, when looking for work as a hay-trusser at Weydon-Priors is to attend the Fair there and have too much furmity[3] to consume. He is with his wife and baby girl, and Hardy comments that it is clear the man and woman are married because of their "atmosphere of stale familiarity". Later Henchard laments that he was a fool to marry at eighteen and that that has caused his current penury. Fuelled by more and more furmity Henchard has his wife and baby auctioned and they are bought by a sailor for five guineas. That all takes place in the first chapter. The next morning, regretting what he had done, though apportioning some blame to the meekness of Susan going along with what he now thinks was a joke and especially regretting the loss of his daughter Elizabeth-Jane, Henchard takes an oath on the Bible that he will not touch strong liquor for twenty-one years "being a year for every year that I have lived."

Of course it is unacceptable to sell one's wife. It is all but unthinkable. Yet under the influence of alcohol hostility is exaggerated, and I am told that incidents of domestic violence increase after important football matches, whether drink is used to celebrate or to drown sorrows. Henchard's behaviour is simply an exaggerated example of the potential behaviour of everyman when drunk. We await, though, Henchard's comeuppance. And indeed more than that, his destruction.

We meet him eighteen years later. He had gone to the far end of Wessex, as far from Weydon-Priors as he could go – somewhere he was not known and the wife-selling too would not be known about. We learn that he has become a successful corn-factor (who has recently sold the millers and bakers poor wheat) and also become Mayor of Casterbridge – both "a great personage" and "a thriving man of business" Hardy writes.

The mistake brought about by furmity is not Henchard's only flaw. He has other unattractive traits or character flaws. He has a temper, very easily acts on impulse, and there is a deal of selfishness and secrecy in his behaviour. *The Mayor of Casterbridge* is a long, complex novel and there is too much of a detailed and well-constructed story for me to outline it. Suffice it to say that Henchard's impulsive behaviour leads to him appointing Donald Farfrae to assist him in his business when he had already promised the job to Joshua Jupp, who had already come across from Jersey specially to take the job, thereby incurring Jupp's enmity which is central to the unmasking of Henchard.

In traditional tragedy there are no obvious winners: Fortinbras and Cassio hold political sway at the end of *Hamlet* and *Othello*, but no-one could place any real confidence in them. With Donald Farfrae, the young Scotsman, by chance passing by on his intended journey from Scotland to Canada, full of contemporary ideas about machinery and agriculture, we have a winner. The crucial point, though, is that he is a winner at the expense of Michael Henchard.

Henchard recognises his abilities and persuades him to stay in Casterbridge, with Farfrae initially helping Henchard, through his expertise in the realm of wheat production, with his business. Subsequently, though, without any malice, Farfrae takes over Henchard's business, marries the woman Henchard is wooing (and has wooed on and off for years) and after her death marries Elizabeth-Jane – and becomes the Mayor of Casterbridge! It is in fact a total triumph for the well-educated modern man as opposed to the poorly educated journeyman hay-trusser.

It is character, though, not social distinctions that more concerns Hardy. In many ways Farfrae is the least complex character in the novel. He is almost too naïve and too good to be true. The Mayor of Casterbridge who matters is Michael Henchard. And he is appropriately complex. I have mentioned some of his weaknesses, but he has strengths too. Yes, he makes bad decisions and rationalises them so that someone else is to blame, but there is no doubting his affection for Elizabeth-Jane, no doubting his responsible behaviour when his sold wife reappears. He also gives food to the poor and provides for the mother of one of his workmen, Abel Whittle. Henchard is a complex character, worthy to be the central hero of a tragedy.

I think that with the plays that I have for the most part been discussing in this series of essays the basic stories are fairly straightforward and so by giving an account of what happens I am not depriving the reader of anything (s)he is unlikely to have some acquaintance with – and certainly not depriving her/him of the excitement of a theatrical experience. With a novel it is different. Reading it is a solitary activity as one turns over the pages and engages with the developing plot and characters. Clearly I want people to read *The Mayor of Casterbridge* and enjoy the unexpected twists and turns of a craftily plotted novel. So I have tried not give too much away and so pre-empt most of the novel's surprises. Mention of Able Whittle, though, leads me to acknowledge how important is the rural scene and life in Hardy's novels. Able Whittle is a lowly worker in Henchard's hay-yard and is frequently late for work. Henchard punishes him for this by insisting he goes to work without his trousers. Whittle, though, remains faithful to his ex-employer and he is the one who is with him at the end and who delivers Henchard's will to Elizabeth-Jane. He symbolises the level to which Henchard had sunk by the end of the novel.

But there are a whole collection of rustics – Coney, Buzzard and Longways are three of them – who meet at the wonderfully named hostelry Peter's Finger in Mixen Lane. They are also responsible for the "skimmity-ride", a pageant through the streets in which effigies of well-known people whose transgressions have become public knowledge are held to ridicule. A pivotal scene in *The Mayor of Casterbridge*. On one level this incident shows the peasants having fun at the expense of their so-called betters, but it is also a comment on the traditional view of the would-be propriety of male-female relationships. Hardy, though, in his treatment of the complexities of human feelings and responsibilities, is very much pushing at the edge of secure establishment values, and at the very least encouraging debate thereon.

The Mayor of Casterbridge is a wonderful novel. It is conducted at a late nineteenth century pace, but once you really get inside Hardy's world, I think you will remain there, entranced by the quality of the writing, the complexity of the plotting and characterisation, the vividness of the scenes depicted – and the sense of the inevitably overriding Fate which dominates all Hardy's serious novels. It is a worldview which he consistently portrays: inescapable.

Michael Henchard, having reached the heights of becoming the Mayor of Casterbridge, is doomed, from his wife-selling in the first chapter, to plummet eventually to the depths of rejected humanity. His will reads:

" 'That Elizabeth-Jane Farfrae be not told of my death, or made to grieve on account of me.
' & that I be not bury'd in consecrated ground.
' & that no sexton be asked to toll the bell.
'& that nobody is wished to see my dead body.
'& that no mourners walk behind me at my funeral.
'& that no flours be planted on my grave.
'& that no man remember me."

J.I.M. Stewart[4] writes: "The man who thought of Aeschylus and Shakespeare ... had an instinct for grounding his fictions in the universal and the permanent, and for establishing their significance in terms of the largest historical perspectives."

Thomas Hardy is some novelist. *The Mayor of Casterbridge* is some novel.

---

[1] This is not evidenced by such things as lists of 100 best novels and so on, but by a sense of every day common consent...

[2] The other four novels in this category are: *Under the Greenwood Tree* (1872), *The Woodlanders* (1887), *Wessex Tales* (1888) and *Life's Little Ironies* (1894).

[3] Furmity or "frumenty" is described by the O.E.D. as "a dish made of hulled wheat, boiled in milk, and seasoned with cinnamon, sugar etc." (harmless enough sounding...!) But in *The Mayor of Casterbridge* the furmity seller, with Henchard's compliance, laces his portions with more and more rum.

[4] in his book *Hardy* (1971)

AUGUST STRINDBERG: *Miss Julie*

Strindberg first gained literary fame at the age of thirty with the publication of what is seen as the first modern Swedish novel *The Red Room*. In the next thirty three years, until his death, he was rarely out of the literary headlines, whether it be as an essayist (frequently political), journalist, novelist, poet or playwright. In addition he was a successful painter: 117 surviving paintings in all, for the most part executed at times of personal stress, and mainly post-Turner seascapes and landscapes. He was both prolific – over sixty plays and more than thirty other various prose works – and multi talented. His prose style is said to have influenced Proust and Kafka, and playwrights such as Tennessee Williams and Edward Albee have expressed a certain debt to him. When Eugene O'Neill accepted his Nobel Prize for Literature in 1936 he was fulsome in his praise for the influence that Strindberg had had on his work and described him as "that greatest genius of all modern dramatists."[1]

Strindberg himself did not win the Nobel Prize. He was favourite to win in 1909 but instead it was awarded to (the now almost unknown) Selma Lagerlof, a fellow Swede and both the first Swede and the first woman to win the award. Maybe it was his anti-establishment views that did not endear him to the Nobel judges. In 1879 he wrote: "I am a socialist, a nihilist, a republican, anything that is anti-reactionary!" Although his lively mind meant he changed his opinions on other issues, that political stance remained pretty constant throughout his life. His main (and changing) influences were Kierkegaard, Brandes, Rousseau, Swedenborg, Nietzsche and, as we shall see particularly with regard to *Miss Julie*, Darwin. He corresponded too with Zola and the artists Munch and Gauguin.

Strindberg probably had the most varied personal experiences of any of the playwrights in this book. My focus is on *Miss Julie* but these are other aspects of his life to be aware of: bankruptcy in the year before the publication of *The Red Room*; three marriages, the latter two to much younger women; early work as a pharmacist, primary school teacher and librarian; death of first child aged two days: lived in both Paris and Berlin; writer's block; depression and mental health breakdown; drink problems especially with regard to absinthe; studied hypnosis and the occult; studied optics, chemistry and botany; and used himself as a guinea pig for psychological and drug-induced experiments. A real polymath, restlessly intellectually engaged throughout his life. Unstable no doubt, but not mad, Strindberg is always worth listening to. I will consider his controversial views on many things (on women and stagecraft perhaps especially) after I have outlined *Miss Julie*.

Miss Julie is a three-hander. It mainly concerns Miss Julie, a twenty-five year old aristocrat and her relationship with her much travelled and knowledgeable servant Jean, who is five years older. There is also the thirty-five year old Kristin to whom Jean is nominally engaged; one assumes that they sleep together as Jean knows that she talks in her sleep, though Kristin adopts a Christian high moral ground towards the end of the play. All the action takes place in the kitchen of the manor house. It is Midsummer's Eve and Kristin has recently broken off her engagement with her fiancé, apparently because he refused to be trained like a dog, breaking Miss Julie's whip the third time she asked him to leap over it. She has consequently not felt in the right mood to accompany her father to the socially appropriate celebrations but has festived with the servants and become the subject of scandalised amusement – "these people aren't slow to jump to conclusions" – as she danced with the gamekeeper and tried to waltz with Jean.

Jean opens a fine bottle of wine from Burgundy which contrasts with the foul smell of what Kristin is cooking – something to cause Miss Julie's dog, Diana, to abort the offspring that the gamekeeper's mutt has sired on her. Jean criticises Miss Julie for her similarities to her mother – being both stuck-up and not taking care "of herself or her person" – but then expresses his admiration: "what a splendid creature." When Miss Julie enters she insists that Jean dances with her, though she adds: "Don't take it as a command. This evening we are all just enjoying ourselves together and any rank is laid aside ... Don't worry, Kristin! I shan't run off with your fiancé!" They leave.

When Jean returns alone he says how crazy Miss Julie is, dancing as she did, and how everyone is guffawing at her. Kristin prosaically suggests that it is "her monthly" and that always makes her act strange. Miss Julie enters. Kristin falls asleep. And Jean changes his livery for a black tail coat and a black derby hat. A long flirtatious dialogue ensues in which Miss Julie attempts to make Jean her plaything: he does, on instruction, kiss her shoe and trembling pleads that "je ne suis qu'un homme", but eventually insists that he will not succumb to being her plaything. Miss Julie, in the course of the dialogue, expresses the view that "everything's strange … Life, people, everything's a scum that drifts, drifts on across the water, until it sinks, sinks…" Miss Julie tells of a dream in which she cannot get down from the pillar which she has climbed, and Jean tells of the poverty of his boyhood. One day, though, he entered the "garden of paradise" of his Lordship's park; he went there with his mother to weed the onion beds, and not only did he see the magnificence of the Turkish pavilion but, hiding under a pile of weeds and thistles that pricked him, he "saw a pink dress and a pair of white stockings." It was Miss Julie and subsequently he washed, put on his best clothes and went to church, just to see Miss Julie. Such was the ecstasy of the vision that, like Keats in his *Ode to a Nightingale* he wished to "cease upon the midnight with no pain." Only Jean's version was to sleep in an oat bin covered with the allegedly dangerous leaves of an elder bush. Obviously he did not die, but he became very ill and realised "how hopeless it was ever to escape from the class in which I was born."

It should be remembered that all this is taking place on Midsummer Night: Shakespeare too employed that night for a night of bewildering love and craziness. Now voices are heard of servants singing "an obscene song … about you and me!" Miss Julie and Jean leave the kitchen – Kristin has already left long ago, pretty well sleepwalking from her chair to the bedroom – and the rollicking peasants enter the kitchen, drink beer and aquavit and sing and dance their obscene, mocking song. The ritual performed, the song over, they leave. While this has been going on, in Jean's room Jean and Miss Julie have had sex, it is implied. Certainly things have changed between them. Perhaps because of the intense mockery, but mainly because of their post-sex situation – "Call me Julie. There are no barriers between us now. Call me Julie" – Jean suggests that they must leave, to Switzerland, to the Italian lakes, somewhere he can start a hotel. It has to be some other country: "There are still barriers between us, as long as we remain in this house." Miss Julie sees it necessary to be taken away "from the shame and the dishonour!"

Arguments then follow. Jean's account of wishing to die in the oat bin was apparently just a story because "women always fall for pretty stories", and when Miss Julie attempts to pull rank again he turns on her: "Lackey's whore, servant's tart ... How dare you call me crude? ... Have you ever seen a girl of my class offer herself like that? I've only seen the like among animals and prostitutes." Jean spells out that there is merely a physical attraction between them and Miss Julie responds "I detest you as I do rats, but I can't run away from you!" Miss Julie then explains her background: how her mother was what we would call a feminist, and she was a commoner. She was prepared to be her father's lover but not his wife, which alienated them from her father's friends. Miss Julie was not a wanted child and her mother's theories meant that women, including Miss Julie, on the estate were put to men's work and vice-versa. Thus her parents became the laughing stock and things fell apart, until her father exerted some form of order. After which the great fire – with arson suspected – burned down all their uninsured property, and money was given by her mother's lover, a brick merchant, to rebuild the house. In this situation her father became very cruel to her mother, Miss Julie sided with her mother who "taught me how to hate men ... and I swore to her that I'd never be a slave to any man." Jean's response is that "I believe you're sick, and your mother was certainly mad." And how he cannot love her because servants cannot be so self-indulgent: "for us love's a game, when work allows." And, probably, together they would "torment each other to death."

Nonetheless Miss Julie takes orders from Jean to get some money (which she steals from her father) in order for them to run away to start a hotel together. Kristin, on her way to church, is disgusted by what she has heard of Miss Julie's behaviour and threatens to put a stop to her "bunking off" with Jean, whereupon Miss Julie suggests she joins them working in their Swiss hotel where "you'll get hold of a husband, a rich Englishman ... they're so easy to catch" This is rejected by Kristin who suggests that Jean "could do with a good sermon after your exploits" and comments on the difficulties of a rich man entering the kingdom of heaven, before leaving and giving instructions that the grooms should not let any horses to Miss Julie and Jean.

Jean had already killed the siskin, Miss Julie's favourite little bird, "the only living creature that loves me now Diana's betrayed me!", and now there seems to be no escape. When Miss Julie's father, the Count, – whose presence, as exemplified by his boots on stage, has never been far away – calls through the speaking tube for his boots and coffee in half an hour, Jean reverts to his role of "damned lackey." Miss Julie is in despair and is given a razor by Jean, the implication being as she walks "resolutely" out through the door, that she will cut her throat.

I hope that outline gives some idea of the energy and the issues to be found in *Miss Julie*. What it does not do is to convey the humour. As with Ibsen and Chekhov Strindberg too writes serious plays, but there is an underlying edgy humour, such as when after Jean has pleaded that "je ne suis qu'un homme", he warns Miss Julie how dangerous it is to play with fire, only for her to respond, "Not for me; I'm insured."

It is the tension between the two main characters that dominates, though. The focus is on male/female relationships and on class in society. The difficulties of relating are at the forefront of many of Strindberg's plays. In *The Father*, for example, in which the Captain has been married to his wife Laura for twenty years, the Nurse comments: "…why do two people have to torture each other to death; two people who are otherwise so good, and so kind to everyone else?" In *The Dance of Death 1*[2], written in 1890 some thirteen years later than *The Father*, the wife, Alice, talks of "our twenty-five years of misery and her husband talks of their having "apparently been condemned to torment each other." Alice refers to "everlasting hell" and almost the last words from her husband are: "I've never been able to figure out whether life is serious or just a joke."

In *Miss Julie* the tension and in-fighting that has lasted for twenty and twenty-five years respectively in *The Father* and *The Dance of*

Death 1 is tautly packed into the events of one night only, Midsummer's Eve. Behind a mutual lust Miss Julie and Jean are vying for supremacy: each is attempting to manipulate the other. (Very like Pinter.) I have mentioned the account Miss Julie gives of her parents' disastrous marriage; there is no doubt that any relationship between Jean and Miss Julie would have been equally disastrous. As it is Jean triumphs, in so far as he survives while Miss Julie commits suicide. In the other two plays I have mentioned, there is, in the one, a limited victory for the woman, in that she does not die, and, in the other, a continuing mutual dependency. Does that make it a draw between the sexes?

No, for Strindberg is particularly hard on women. Scathing at times. In his *Preface* to *Miss Julie* (which I shall discuss further later) he, without apparently a second thought or a cavil, writes: "Jean... is superior to Miss Julie in that he is man." And Kurt in *The Dance of Death 1* says to Alice "you're the first woman I've ever felt sorry for, all the others seemed to me to deserve what they got." In a long speech at the beginning of Scene 7 of *The Father* the captain explains why his mother, his sister, his first lover, his daughter and his wife have, for different reasons, all been his enemies. "A curse upon all your sex!" he calls at the end of the play, in which all the way through he has been lamenting that paternity can never be proved. His wife Laura says that "love between the sexes is a battle" – a battle which she wins!

But is all this misogyny or an adoption of a viewpoint for the sake of the drama? For in 1884 – *Miss Julie* was written in 1888 – Strindberg was advocating women's suffrage. However years later he completely reversed that viewpoint, calling for the removal of the vote from these "half-apes ...mad... criminal, instinctively evil animals." You could argue that this latter view was expressed at a time when Strindberg was experiencing a time of mental instability, but, having said that, there is not a little resonance with how he portrays women in the plays I have mentioned.[3] (Although with the plays Strindberg was adamant that no autobiographical elements[4] should be read into them.) Perhaps we should leave it there. The question of Strindberg's attitude to women (which implies the hopeless weakness of men) will always be debated.[5]

Miss Julie too is after all half-man/half-woman. She does not know where she emotionally stands, as a result of her parents and her recently dismissed fiancé. She is unsure of who she is – except that she is an aristocrat. And therein lies the source of any power she has over Jean. Initially Jean, albeit hesitantly, will obey the order to kiss Miss Julie's foot, but as the play goes on it is clear who gains the supremacy. By the end, as Jean explains to Kristin "they're no better than we are", Miss Julie is taking the order from him, to rob her father. There is a Darwinian theme which, Strindberg's *Preface* avers, is being explored. He writes of a "life and death" evolutionary struggle for the fittest to survive. Miss Julie is an aristocratic throwback, with no survival skills in the modern world, whereas Jean has survival skills and is adaptable. Yet clearly, in Strindberg's presentation, the world of 1888 was not poised for revolution, as, on hearing his master's voice, Jean automatically reverts, reluctantly, to his servant role: "I believe if his lordship came down now and ordered me to cut my throat I'd do it on the spot." Strindberg adds, however, in the *Preface*: "(Jean's) inferiority arises mainly from the social milieu in which he temporarily finds himself and which he will probably discard along with his livery."

So the thoughts of Marx and Darwin were explored in Strindberg's plays. What about the other great nineteenth-century thinker, Freud? He had not read Freud when *Miss Julie* was written, but the theories of the neurologist Breuer (with whom Freud collaborated) about the use of hypnosis and the treatment of hysteria were prevalent. There was a psychological zeitgeist which any intelligent alive thinker, as Strindberg unquestionably was, would tap into. With the result that he refuses to give Miss Julie one simplistic motivation. "I have motivated Miss Julie's tragic fate with an abundance of circumstances," he asserts, and proceeds to list fourteen intertwined circumstances. He sees this "multiplicity of motives as being "in tune with the times." For Strindberg Miss Julie is a Naturalistic symbol of degeneration, always going to fail the struggle in which she finds herself as, in addition to being a passe aristocrat, she is a woman who will never catch up with a man "neither with the help of equal education, equal voting rights, disarmament or temperance – no more than two parallel lines can ever meet or cross."

I have strayed again, perhaps inevitably, into the battle of the sexes – Strindberg is so full of it! But a few words about his theory of the theatre. Writing *Miss Julie* he was in his Naturalism phase. This was by-and-large borrowed from Zola's "la nouvelle formule", with its three fundamental principles: that the work should be grounded in psychological realism, with due acknowledgement to both heredity and environment, and in a realistic setting; the conflicts fought should be significantly life-changing; and these should be focused and simple, with no distracting subplots. *Miss Julie* would seem to fulfil these requirements, though Zola, who was less a fan of Strindberg than Strindberg was of him, did complain that Strindberg's figures lacked "a complete social setting." And indeed in comparison with the wonderfully detailed backgrounds that Zola gives his characters that is undoubtedly true. But Strindberg's naturalistic approach is also seen in his allowing his characters' "brains to wander irregularly as they do in real life" so that the dialogue wanders. In his *Preface* Strindberg links his play with classical theatre with his use of monologue, mime and ballet "in order to provide resting places for the audience and the actors." He also suggest a single set, with no need for expensive scenery and suggests that "in a modern psychological drama, where the subtlest movements of the soul should be mirrored more in the face than in gestures and words, it would probably be best to experiment with strong side lighting on a small stage and with actors wearing no make-up, or at least a bare minimum." No footlights he suggested too.

This is Strindberg immersed in how to most powerfully present his psychological theatre. In later life he had much more revolutionary views about the theatre. He distanced himself from naturalism in 1889 in an essay "*On Modern Drama and the Modern Theatre*" in which he described naturalism as petty and unimagenative realism. In 1900 he wrote the experimental *A Dream Play* in which he wrote that he "attempted to imitate the inconsequent yet apparently logical form of a dream." Neither time nor place exists while "the imagination spins and weaves new patterns." It is the dreamer whose consciousness holds sway over everything, and we the audience are the dreamer as we witness Agnes, the daughter of the Vedic god Indra, descend to earth and have encounters with some forty people. It is an exciting imaginative achievement and clearly predates and encourages Surrealism.

Yes, Strindberg was a polymath, a great exploratory mind with links to insanity and there were years when, although writing poetry and novels and essays for journals, he did not write for the theatre. But his lasting reputation is as a playwright and a theorist of dramaturgy. He founded The Intimate Theatre in Stockholm in 1907, for which he wrote chamber plays, of which the best known is *The Ghost Sonata* (1907), which has stylistic links with *A Dream Play*; he sees it too as "chamber music transposed to drama" and gave his four chamber plays an Opus number. The stage for The Intimate Theatre was a mere six by nine metres; there were only 160 seats; there was no restaurant but there was a smoking room for the gentlemen and a lounge for the ladies; no liquor was sold and there were no Sunday performances; no intermissions either. All interesting ideas, though Strindberg died in 1912 believing that no play of his had been staged exactly as he wanted it to be.

The point, though, is that he was a very serious dramatist and theatre-theorist. I see him primarily, through *Miss Julie* as a brilliant psychological dramatist. He links too with the Greeks as he writes of Miss Julie being the "victim of the errors of an age, of circumstances, and of her own deficient constitution, which together form the equivalent of the old-fashioned concept of Fate or Universal law." In terms of the position of women in the late nineteenth century she was a tragic heroine par excellence. And has anyone written better than Strindberg about the inescapable conflicts between men and women?

---

[1] Note too Sean O'Casey's comment in a letter: "Strindberg, Strindberg, Strindberg, the greatest of them all… Barrie sits mumbling as he silvers his little model stars and gilds his little model suns, while Strindberg shakes flame from the living planets and the fixed stars. Ibsen can sit serenely in his Doll's House, while Strindberg is battling with his heaven and his hell.

Continued…

[2] There is a *Dance of Death 11*, much less frequently performed, but, with the same characters, written as a sequel after a positive response to the first play.

[3] It is believed that Miss Julie and her fate is based on the Swedish novelist Victoria Benedictsson, also dressed and brought up as a boy, who too cut her throat with a razor.

[4] It is true, however, that at the time of writing *The Father* he was deeply troubled with doubts about his own paternity.

[5] Strindberg's alleged anti-Semitism will also always be debated, though this is not relevant to *Miss Julie*.

HENRIK IBSEN:
Hedda Gabler and *The Master Builder*

Ibsen is the second most performed playwright in the world – after Shakespeare. In all he wrote twenty-five plays, the last sixteen of which, commencing with *Brand* written in 1866 and concluding with *When We Dead Awaken* in 1899, can frequently be seen on the contemporary stage. There is no doubting his stature as a playwright and his ability to assiduously craft memorable plays on memorable themes with memorable parts for actors – Hedda Gabler, for example, has been played in recent years by Ingrid Bergman, Jill Bennett, Janet Suzman (my personal favourite), Glenda Jackson, Diana Rigg, Isabelle Hupert, Claire Bloom, Fiona Shaw, Harriet Walter, Cate Blanchett and, most recently, Sheridan Smith.

Yet when his plays were first produced in the United Kingdom there was an almost universal vitriolic hostile reception. *The Daily Telegraph* reported on *The Master Builder*: "One may compare it ... to the sensation of a man who witnesses a play written, rehearsed and acted by lunatics." *The Globe* critic said of it: "Platitudes and inanities... The play is hopeless and indefensible" and *The Stage* critic referred to "Three Acts of gibberish." *The Pall Mall Gazette* wrote of the main female character: "Hilda Wangel is perhaps the most detestable character in the drama's range ... victim of nymphomania ... deliberate murderess." It was not just the English press which descended on Ibsen: Strindberg – for what might be seen as reasons of envy or impending madness – called Ibsen "a decrepit old troll" writing "shit". And Chekhov questioned Ibsen's knowledge of real life.

The main reason for this critical vilification is that Ibsen was a revolutionary in the theatre, bringing social realism in particular and also psychological exploration to a theatre which hitherto had had a staple diet of comedies or verse plays[1]. Ibsen wrote in prose. And despite the critics Ibsen's plays were admired by many fellow writers, including Thomas Hardy, Henry James and, especially, George Bernard Shaw. Shaw and Ibsen shared similar left-wing political views, though Ibsen was far less a proponent of his views than was Shaw. Indeed Ibsen was criticised for not joining a political party, but he was not into conventional politics, though acknowledging that his views were left of centre and radical. His friend Georg Brandes wrote of Ibsen "(his) whole character presupposes a distrust of and ill-will towards parliamentarianism. He believes in the individual, in the single great personality; the individual, and he alone, can accomplish everything.[2] Such a body as parliament is, in Ibsen's eyes, a mere assembly of orators and dilettanti." It is a "revolution of the spirit" to which Ibsen aspires.

In Hedda Gabler Ibsen has created a woman who has lost her raison d'être. Hilda Wangel in *The Master Builder* is very much in touch with the revolution of the spirit – not so Hedda Gabler. That name is important. When the play begins she is six months into her marriage with George Tesman, but she keeps her father's name, her father who was a General and whose portrait hangs on the living room wall, perhaps dominating the stage and, at the very least, a presence that the audience is never allowed to forget. He has bequeathed his daughter a love of riding and of pistols which is way beyond the academic world of her husband. And Hedda is bored. She has married Tesman as an acknowledgment that the more exciting days of her youth are over, and he has been assiduously attentive in such things as walking her home after parties. He has been a safe pair of hands, though conversation between them has not always been easy and, once for want of something to say, she has professed to having always admired the house they are now living in. So when, fortuitously, it came on the market, Tesman bought it. In fact Hedda has no special feelings for it and it is a house whose mortgage and upkeep they cannot afford.

Their honeymoon has lasted six months and, during it, Tesman has continued to research his new book on the domestic industries of Brabant during the Middle Ages. It is difficult to stifle a yawn just reading that subject, never mind having to live with it every day for six months. What about their sex life? Some critics have suggested that Hedda is pregnant, others that the marriage has not been consummated. Either way what is true is that Hedda is totally unresponsive to Tesman's Aunt Julia's hints about the possibility of a baby, and being a father to a baby – as distinct from giving birth to a book – is clearly not on Tesman's mind. I believe that the marriage has been unsatisfactorily consummated and sex has become an occasional chore for Hedda that she prefers not to think about and is a part of her disillusionment at the situation in which she finds herself.

Ibsen, in Hedda Gabler, has given us a realistic portrait of a romantic woman. One of her past lovers is Eilert Lovborg. He is an old academic rival of Tesman's who until recently had had a major drink problem, but under the guidance of Thea Elvsted he has broken the alcohol dependency and has, again with Thea's help, just published a very well received book on the march of civilisation. It becomes clear that Thea Elvsted is in love with Eilert Lovborg and has left her considerably older husband and followed Lovborg to town (Kristiana). Hedda and Thea knew each other at school: Hedda claims it was a friendly relationship but, almost certainly correctly, Thea remembers Hedda as a frightening bully who threatened to both cut off her hair and to burn it off her head. Hedda is far from being a nice person – but then neither was Faustus or Macbeth or Rigoletto et al.

Mrs Elvsted, as she is more commonly called in *Hedda Gabler*, is worried that Lovborg will fall into the laps of other attractive women in town, and the only people in Kristiana she knows and can ask for help from are Tesman, with who she once had a short-lived fling, and Hedda Gabler. Hedda ruthlessly exploits Mrs Elvsted's dependency. She is jealous of the Lovborg-Elvsted relationship and not only wants to break it up but she wants Lovborg to be the romantic young man she remembers and has a recurrent vision of him "with vine leaves in his hair"[3]. There is an exciting dynamic between Hedda and Lovborg: together she reminds him that "there was really something beautiful, something fascinating – something daring –in – in – that secret intimacy – that comradeship which no living creature so much as dreamed of." For them that was love, in total contrast to the relationship Hedda has with Tesman and, for that matter, the one that Lovborg has with Mrs Elvsted. Hedda will not demean herself by committing adultery, but she wants to reclaim the power she once had over

Lovborg and, eventually she taunts him into having a glass of punch and then going off with Tesman to what will undoubtedly be a drinking party at Judge Brack's house.

True enough, Lovborg goes off the rails: "he is incapable of taking his pleasure in moderation," says Tesman. So the next morning he does not return with Tesman. Tesman, though, has found the "whole of his precious irreplaceable manuscript,"[4] Lovborg's new book which was his real work and destined to be a triumph and been inspired by a woman unnamed. Tesman leaves the manuscript with Hedda.

When a confused and irritated Lovborg eventually arrives at the Tesman's house, he believes he has lost forever the manuscript and breaks off his relationship with Mrs Elvsted, telling her that he has ripped it into pieces and agreeing that he has destroyed their child. Ashamed after his night of "riot and debauchery" Lovborg wants to "make an end to it all" and Hedda gives him one of General Gabler's pair of pistols insisting that he does it "beautifully". Hedda, enjoying the electricity of power and writing her own script, has not told Lovborg that she has the manuscript safely in her possession. And, after he has gone, she proceeds, quire by quire, to throw it into the burning stove, relishing burning the child of Eilert Lovborg and Thea Elvsted. The drama does not end there. Lovborg does shoot himself with Hedda's pistol, but he does not die a "beautiful and free" death, with vine leaves in his hair, as Hedda had envisaged. In fact it is a "ridiculous and vile" death: he shoots himself, just perhaps accidentally, in the bowels in a brothel in the boudoir of Mlle Diana, where he returned still seeking his manuscript. "Oh, what curse is it that makes everything I touch turn ludicrous and mean" laments Hedda. And while Tesman and Mrs Elvsted are seeing if they can maybe reconstruct Lovborg's lost manuscript from a few papers and memory – "arranging other people's papers is just the work for me," says Tesman – another shot rings out.

Eleven years earlier in *A Doll's House* a door slammed and a would-be independent woman walked out on her husband and children. Now it is a pistol shot which shatters the theatre and another woman has found what she conceives as the only way out from her totally unsatisfactory life. Hedda's life was about to become even more impossible: Judge Brack knows it was her pistol with which Lovborg killed himself, which puts her henceforth in his power; and Tesman has built an exuberant hope for the future on Hedda for once having called him George. But it is not just the encroaching circumstances that cause Hedda Gabler to commit suicide with a bullet through her temple. Her own romanticism and excruciating boredom made it inevitable. Maybe in a previous century she could have been a lady at court, maybe today she would resort to high class drugs. But nothing would have satisfied her for long. She sees beauty and courage in suicide, "a deed worth doing."

Obviously suicide is not the answer to all loveless marriages. It is an extreme way out and Hedda is an extreme case. In that way she is – however unlovable she may be – an archetype, a representative of womankind, encouraging us to find our own ways to put an end to despair and misery in marriage. Hedda Gabler continues to hold a fascination for us. In popular culture there is a prostitute called Hedda Gobbler in Michael Winterbottom's 2005 film, starring Steve Coogan and Rob Bryden, *Tristram Shandy: A Cock and Bull Story*, and in Helen Fielding's 2013 novel *Bridget Jones: Mad About the Boy* the eponymous heroine is trying in a very uninformed manner to write a modern version of the play. And the Iranian translator and director of *Hedda Gabler*, Vahid Rahbani, was taken to court and the production of the play stopped after an Iranian news agency reviewed it as "vulgar" and "hedonistic" with "symbols of sexual slavery cult." I don't understand where that last comment comes from, but the point is that *Hedda Gabler* continues to make waves wherever it is performed. Both as a symbol of disaffected womankind and as a realistic portrait Hedda Gabler is some woman!

Hedda Gabler is usually seen as the end of Ibsen's realistic series of plays that had begun with *Pillars of Society*[5]. *The Master Builder*, written in the year following *Hedda Gabler*, is seen as inaugurating Ibsen's final more symbolic phase of play-writing. To some extent, but only to some extent this is true – it could equally be argued that he is returning to the symbolism of Brand and Peer Gynt which is found in his earlier plays. Ibsen's plays cannot be fitted into neat self-contained boxes. For in all his plays the characters have a convincing psychologically realistic element in them, the later plays being no exception. As Ibsen himself wrote: "I have often walked with Hedda Gabler in the Munich arcades" – a remark, I think also relevant to both Master Builder Solness and Hilda Wangel.

I do want to explore both the symbolism and the autobiographical material which is always intriguing about *The Master Builder*, but it is important to register how plausible are Ibsen's characters. Many of his contemporaries, cloaking themselves in a conservative Victorian morality, did not think[6] so but then the ideas of Freud has not burst upon the intellectual scene. It is remarkable that Ibsen anticipates Freud – Freud's first published work, *Studies in Hysteria* did not appear until 1895, by which time Ibsen had written fourteen of his sixteen major plays. Ibsen was fully aware of the importance of symbolism **and** of inner driving forces that have their own particular and personal logic. Apparently his way of working was to map out a plot and then do a first draft when he was making the acquaintance of his characters, when they were like first-time met companions on a train journey, and then a second draft by which time they were beginning to be well-known and, finally a third draft – the plots never changed, but the characters did. So, without further discussion, let us grant that Ibsen knows the psychology of his characters and that they are all realistic portraits. That is true of Master Builder Solness and Hilda Wangel. Which means that we can turn to the autobiographical elements in the story and to the symbolism.

Ibsen never distances himself from his characters: there is always a personal involvement in his plays. Perhaps none more so than with Master Builder Halvard Solness. In the first place Ibsen saw himself as constructing his plays in the manner of architectural work. Secondly, addressing students he admitted that Solness was "a man somewhat akin to me." Thirdly, Ibsen too had a fear of great heights. Fourthly, and arguably most importantly, was the inspiration Ibsen took from younger women.

There was Helene Raff who told Ibsen the story of the architect of St Michael's Church in Munich who had fallen to his death when climbing the church to place a crowning celebratory wreath on the spire, and to whom Ibsen, understandably, sent a signed copy of *The Master Builder*. Later there was Hildur Andersen, whom Ibsen met when she was ten and who became his companion when she was twenty-seven and he was sixty-three. Their first meeting was in 1864. But it is the young woman he met in 1889, two years before the first production of *The Master Builder*, to whom most attention has been give. Emilie Bardach was her name: she was Austrian and she was eighteen at the time (Ibsen was sixty-one). They met in Gossenas where Ibsen was summering; a square had been named after him on a steep hill, and Ibsen puffed his way up it for the naming ceremony. After the ceremony they talked and then again at a birthday party where Emilie recorded "we understood each other so well." During his stay Ibsen was very attentive and they continued to correspond until Ibsen broke off the relationship, claiming that he was being unfair to a young woman who should be involved in different things. There was no doubt, though, about the delight both experienced in the relationship: Ibsen wrote in Emilie's album a quotation from Goethe's *Faust*: "Oh, high and painful joy – to struggle for the unattainable!" And when the silence between the two was broken after seven years by Emilie sending a seventieth birthday congratulatory telegram, he replied: "…the summer in Gossenas was the happiest, the most beautiful in my whole life. I scarcely dare to think of it – and yet I must think of it always. Always! Your truly devoted, H.I." As an older woman, eighty-six in fact, Emilie Bardach went on record to say that she and Ibsen had never even kissed. Some have attempted to sully Ibsen's name with hints of paedophilia, but many a teacher, for example, has felt his/her life enriched and energised by contact with a younger student without there ever being even a hint of sexual impropriety. What is true is that there is no doubt that Emilie represented what Ibsen always sought, a longing for "livsglaede", the joy of life.

And she was, in altered form, the inspiration behind Hilda Wangel. When she first saw the play Emilie's comment was: "I didn't see myself, but I saw him. There is something of me in Hilda; but in Solness, there is little that is not Ibsen." I find it fascinating to trace Ibsen's life's connection with his plays – how much, for example, can we read into the picture of the Solness's marriage as a commentary on Ibsen's own? But maybe I have been sidetracked down the path of biography too far and it really is time to consider the play. (And for any reader interested in the life of Ibsen there is a biography written by Michael Meyer in 1967, which is both thoroughly researched and well-written, and from which I have taken most of the above biographical material.)

Halvard Solness has flaws. Who doesn't? Only gods have the possibility of perfection. He is insecure, frightened of the younger generation knocking at the door and usurping him, just as he usurped his previous employer, Knut Brovik, "formerly an architect, now in Solness's employment". Brovik's son, Ragnor, is also employed by Solness as a draughtsman and Solness's bookkeeper is Kaia Fosli, cousin to Ragnor and engaged to marry him. Ragnor has ambitions, and almost certainly the talent, to design houses himself but, until Hilda Wangel comes along, Solness will not free him, and, in order to ensure that Ragnor remains working for him, Solness has manufactured a romantic liaison between himself and Kaia: she says that now she cannot care for anyone else and Solness, before kissing her hair, professes that "I must have you with me every single day." He is using both of them so that he can be given the credit of building his "home for happy men." But once Hilda had re-entered his life he frees and dismisses both Ragnor and Kaia. He no longer has any use for them.

Before we discuss the central relationship in *The Master Builder*, that between Solness and Hilda, there is how Solness came to be a success and his marriage to be considered – both of which throw substantial light on his character. His success came as a result of a fire in the Solness's family home: the home was completely destroyed and he was able to lay out "almost the whole of the garden in villa lots" and build his homes for human beings. In the course of explaining all this to Hilda, Solness admits to being self-taught and not having taken the necessary exams to enable him to call himself an architect. Again deep-down insecurity. But what is perhaps more significant is that he believes that he willed the fire. He knew there was a crack in the chimney and he ignored repairing it, and the "great, dark, ugly wooden box" with the great garden, inherited from his wife's mother was burned to the ground. Solness has his wish and out of that wish-fulfilment has come his good reputation, his building of social housing for families. To him it matters not that the faulty chimney had nothing to do with the fire. He feels a certain responsibility and hence guilt. In addition he believes that, subconsciously, he can make things happen – and he links the arrival of Hilda with this perceived attribute.

The fire was responsible too for another loss for Solness and his wife, Aline: their twin boys, scarcely three weeks old. They did not die in the fire itself, but as a result of Aline post-fire falling into a fever which poisoned her breast milk on which the boys fed. Aline lost not only their children and the chance of having more children, but also her family home, with the portraits of past generations – she felt orphaned. She actually expresses more grief for the loss of nine little dolls she had kept from her childhood than she does for the twin boys. She is a desperately unhappy woman (and completely aware of Solness's heavy flirting with Kaia) and burdens her husband with: "You may do all the building in the world. Halvard – for me you can never build a real home again." Weighed down by insecurity, responsibility and guilt, "terribly afraid of the younger generation", Solness needs a blast of energy, of hope in his life – some excitement. Enter Hilda Wangel.

In fact she enters on cue. Somewhat cornily, but dramatically effective, just as Solness says, "presently the younger generation will come knocking at my door" Hilda knocks. Ten years ago, when Hilda was fourteen, they had become acquainted, in Lysanger when Solness had laid a wreath on the recently repaired church tower. She remembers his singing on the church tower and having an impassioned talk with him, during which he had called her "a little princess" and promised that he would return in ten years and buy her the kingdom of Orangia. She also has a memory of being bent back by Solness and being kissed many times. Ten years have elapsed and Solness has not fulfilled his promise, so here she is to claim her kingdom. Solness has no recollection of any of this. All he remembers is a "little devil in white" shouting "hurrah for the master builder" down below, thereby distracting him and almost causing him to fall. Since then he has given in to his acrophobia and never climbed a tower again, and has built homes for people and not for God. For ten years Hilda has built on her impressionable teenage fantasies; when furious with Solness's lack of contact she has occasionally been "interested in other people for a week or so", but she has always returned to her yearning for the Master Builder and for him to fulfil the promises she believes he made.

"Each man hears what he wants to hear and disregards the rest."[7]. That clearly has been the case with both Hilda and Solness. But there is something about Hilda that reinvigorates Solness. He responds to her suggestions, knowing that he might well be "half-mad" or "crazy". Eventually he responds to her pleading with him to do the impossible and to "stand free and high up", recreating the image she has had of him for ten years. She finds it all so "frightfully thrilling" and when he climbs up the scaffolding with his wreath to place it on the weather-vane at the top of the new house, she calls out again "Hurrah for Master Builder Solness". We know that two workers have already fallen and been "killed on the spot." Solness too falls to his death, and Hilda has the last words: "My – my Master Builder."

Before Solness's death Hilda has demanded her castle in the air, and Solness has promised her that "after this day we two will build together" and though it will be a real castle in the air it will have, says Solness, "a firm foundation under it." Romantic, lovers' talk. They have agreed that one cannot choose whom one is going to be fond of and that is ruled by "the troll within."[8] In truth they are both behaving like crazy romantics – Solness is completely in thrall to his own belle dame sans merci.

In both characters and situation we have realism. In both characters and situation we have romanticism. In addition we have symbolism. An older man is trying to impress a much younger woman, responding to her possessive hero-worship[9]. He therefore attempts to do something that is beyond him and falls from a great height. Once up he cannot sustain his position. His fear of the younger generation has been amply justified. And what does the memorable symbol of the fall say about love? Stendhal made the beautiful comment that every lover's passion is a flower above a frightful abyss – the heights are exhilarating but the depths await. This is the Master Builder's experience, graphically and symbolically presented. Ibsen knew what he was writing about, but he sublimated his feelings for Emilie Bardach (and other young, energising, inspiring women) into *The Master Builder*.

I hope I have conveyed something of the greatness of Ibsen. Both Hedda Gabler and Halvard Solness are characters of distinction for whom a tragic fate awaits. I am aware that there is so much more to

Ibsen than I have outlined. In *The Master Builder*, for example I have not mentioned the childhood dreams of Ibsen that impacted on the play, nor have I discussed – as Solness does – Solness's relationship with God. And the trolls play a significant part too. Also there is humour. The plays are serious but it always surprises me how his detailed characterisation produces so many laughs in the theatre.

Let me conclude with the words of Pirandello: "After Shakespeare, without hesitation, I put Ibsen first.

---

[1] "…It is not the least of Ibsen's numerous contributions to the theatre that he turned it from a place of entertainment and occasional catharsis into a place from which men emerged compelled to rethink basic principles which they had never before seriously questioned. (*Ibsen*: Michael Meyer.)

[2] Romantic and realist alike are attracted to Ibsen's plays!

[3] Amongst artistic circles in Rome it was customary for revellers to deck themselves thus.

[4] Losing a manuscript is based on the real life experience of Julius Hoffory, a Danish Professor of Philology with whom Ibsen was well acquainted.

[5] The three major earlier plays – *Brand, Peer Gynt* and *Emperor and Galilean* are poetic and, latterly, historical – and there is a six year gap before *Pillars of Society*.

[6] Her Majesty's censor, a Mr Pigott, thought all Ibsen's characters "morally deranged."

[7] In the words of Paul Simon.

[8] To live is to battle with troll folk
In the crypts of heart and head.
To write is a man's self-judgment,
As doom shall judge the dead… (Henrik Ibsen)

[9] There are parallels here with Hedda Gabler's response to Eilert Lovborg.

ANTON CHEKHOV: *The Seagull*

Chekhov, the author too of some of the world's best short stories, wrote five major plays: *Ivanov* (1887), *The Seagull* (1896), *Uncle Vanya* (1897)[1], *The Three Sisters* (1901) and *The Cherry Orchard* (1904). There were some early one Act plays also, but the main focus on all his plays has to be on the latter four, which are still frequently to be seen in theatres throughout the world.

The plays were popular at the Moscow Art Theatre in Chekhov's lifetime, although the first night of *The Seagull* – at the Alexandrinsky Theatre – was a disaster. Nina's monologue, part of a play in which she is performing, about "all living things having completed their mournful cycle" and she being "the common soul of the world", was jeered at and ridiculed – and this set the tone for the audience's response. The actress playing Nina, faced with this hostility, lost her voice, and Chekhov left his place in the audience after the second Act and walked the streets of Petersburg until two in the morning and vowed never to write another play! In fact *The Seagull* was much better received on the second night and subsequently, though the management did, after a short run, accede to Chekhov's request to take it off. 1898, however, saw the founding of the Moscow Art Theatre and Stanislavsky directed *The Seagull*. The play had twenty-six rehearsals, only one of which was attended by Chekhov, who, when asked how a particular part should be played unhelpfully answered "as well as possible." It cannot be overestimated how important this production of *The Seagull* was to the Moscow Art Theatre: this was its fourth production, and although the first production[2] had been a success, this had been followed by the failure of the second play[3] and the third planned play being banned. Another failure could prove to be a nail in the coffin of a young theatre. Chekhov had nervously fled to Yalta for the winter and his sister Maria implored the management not to stage the play, fearing for her brother's health. But it went ahead. Stanislavsky reported what happened: at the end of the first Act, when the curtain came down, there was total silence. Olga Knipper – playing Madam Arkadina[4] – was close to sobbing, when a great ring of applause broke out. Chekhov's other career – he was a practising doctor – as a playwright was secured.

The Seagull had worked on stage. It was largely due to the quality of the writing, as Chekhov, by understatement, realistically conveyed the ennui and wry melancholic failure at the core of each character's lonely life. It was everyday life that he was depicting, so perhaps some credit could also go to Stanislavsky who, in his directorial score published in 1938, detailed when actors should "wipe away dribble, blow their noses, wipe away sweat, or clean their teeth or nails with matchsticks."

The plays were translated into English between 1908 and 1916. And they appealed to George Bernard Shaw. What attracted Shaw was the presentation in all Chekhov's plays of an aimless society drifting towards its own destruction. In 1919 Shaw wrote *Heartbreak House*: set just before the outbreak of World War 1, the play depicts different strata of upper and upper-middle class people who have no understanding of and are indifferent to both the likely impact of a World War and the working classes. (I am tempted to say "plus ça change…") There is a working class girl, Ellie, in the play too. Shaw is satirising this group of people, but where Shaw cannot hold a candle to Chekhov is in his characterisation. Where Shaw's characters are one-dimensional and pretty well caricatures, Chekhov's have a real inner life. And where Shaw is focused on ridiculing the class-ridden society he depicts, with Chekhov we have a sympathetic human understanding.

Leaving aside – just for the moment – the major question of whether Chekhov's plays are comedies or tragedies, let me tell the story of *The Seagull*, and that narrative, I believe, will lead us in a certain direction. A family country estate is the setting for all four Acts. Sorin, a retired civil servant in ill health, lives there as head of the family, though, as he moans: "I've retired now, I've got nowhere to go. I've got to live here, whether I want to or not…" His sister, Arkadina, a renowned actress is visiting with her current lover Trigorin, a well-known writer: the former is described by her son Trepliov as needing constant praise and acclaim and being tight-fisted with money, and he describes Trigorin as being "a long way off forty" whose writing is "very clever and charming."

Trepliov is himself a budding playwright and an assembled audience begins to watch a futuristic play of his which has a young neighbour called Nina,[5] with whom Trepliov is in love, in the lead part. It is a revolutionary play, being "dreams of things as they will be two hundred thousand years from now." Before the play begins Nina has commented that "there's hardly any action in your play, there are only speeches", and Arkadina's constant ridiculing of the play causes her son to furiously bring down a very early curtain. Amongst those also watching the play are Medvienko, a dull middle-aged pedantic teacher lamenting what a hard life teaching is, Dorn a wordly-wise doctor who alone praises Trepliov's play, and, perhaps most significantly, Masha, the daughter of the bailiff who runs the estate: she is in love with Trepliov and sets the tone of the play right at the beginning of the first Act by always wearing black because "I am in mourning for my life. I'm unhappy." Towards the end of Act 1 Arkadina comments on the looks and lovely voice of Nina and adds: "you really ought not to stay in the country... You must go on the stage!" Nina replies: "Oh, it's my one dream. But it'll never come true."

Act 2 of *The Seagull* takes place at midday by a croquet lawn a few days later. Again Masha sets the mood by admitting that "often I don't feel like going on with life at all." Arkadina gives her some self-righteous advice, again saying that "while you stay in the same place all the time, you don't really live." Then Arkadina has a row with Masha's father, the bailiff: about horses – whether their use for trips to the town is more important than their necessary employment on the farm "carting the rye", and she determines to leave immediately. Trepliov finds Nina alone and lays at her feet a dead seagull which he was "despicable enough to kill." He warns that he will kill himself in the same way and is distressed that Nina seems to be moving away from him, and, when "the real genius" Trigorin is seen approaching, he departs quickly. A long – and, I think, rather tedious – discussion about Trigorin and his art and attitude to it and himself ensues. Nina comments that for fame, as an actress, she would put up with all kinds of deprivations and dissatisfaction with herself. Trigorin notices the dead seagull and sees it as "A subject for a short story: a young girl, like you, has lived beside a lake from childhood. She loves the lake as a seagull does, and she's happy and free as a seagull. But a man chances to come along, sees her, and having nothing better to do, destroys her, just like this seagull here." The Act concludes with Arkadina announcing that, after all, they are staying and Nina ambiguously reflecting "It's a dream!"

Act 3 sees, at last, the departure of Arkadina and Tregorin for Moscow. Masha again sets the Chekhovian mood at the start of the Act by telling Tregorin that she is going to marry the schoolteacher Medvedenko for: "What is the point of love without hope, of waiting whole years for something … one doesn't know what …But when I'm married there'll be no time for love." We learn that Trepliov has shot himself in the head, though the bullet only grazed his skull. His mother cannot understand why he should try to kill himself, and her brother, an increasingly ill Sorin, suggests that he's living in the country "with no money, no position, no future" and that he probably feels like "a cadger, living on charity." Sorin suggests she give her son money to buy some new clothes and have some fun and Trepliov suggests to his mother that her brother's health would improve if she were to lend Sorin two thousand roubles so he could spend a year in town: both suggestions are turned down pretty peremptorily as her dress-bill alone "is enough to ruin me." The other major development is that Nina has clearly now fallen for Tregorin: she presents him with a medallion with a reference to page 121 lines 11 and 12 of his book *Days and Nights*, which reads "if ever you need my life, come and take it." Tregorin's response is to ask Arkadina to release him as all the time he is possessed by "sweet and wonderful dreams" of Nina. Arkadina then plays two trump cards that, at least for the moment, bind Tregorin to her: that she will go out of her mind if he leaves her and that she sees him as the best of all modern writers and "I alone know how to appreciate you." So they go back to Moscow together – but not before Nina and Tregorin enjoy a prolonged kiss as they plan to meet again in Moscow where Nina has determined to pursue an acting career.

Masha is again prominent at the opening of the last Act. It is two years later and she has had a baby with Medvedenko, who she now can't bear the sight of; she still, however feels love for Trepliov, which leads her to philosophise: "If love sneaks into your heart the best thing to do is to chuck it out." Nina does not articulate the same thought, but the other characters, talking about her, reveal that she had an affair and a child with Trigorin in Moscow, but the child died and Trigorin went back to Arkadina. Trepliov has followed her career as an actress and explains that "there were moments when she showed talent ... but they were only moments." She now acts in the provinces, and she corresponds with Trepliov, signing herself "Seagull". Trepliov is having some success with his story writing, but Arkadina still has not had time to have read anything written by her son. (She has been telegraphed to come to the family estate because Sorin is deemed to be dying.) Most of this talk, this revealing of what has been happening in the intervening two years, takes place against the background of a game of bingo, but when all but Trepliov leave for supper, he hears a tapping at the window. It is Nina. Trepliov tells her that "I was bound to your heart and soul for ever. It's not in my power to stop loving you" and that he is lonely. Nina expresses how tired she is and reminisces about their play. Twice she says "I am a seagull" and her comment on life, before she runs out through the French window to travel in a third-class carriage to act in Yelietz, is: "what really matters is not fame, or glamour ...but knowing how to endure things. How to bear one's cross and have faith." Trepliov then tears up all his manuscripts and departs. A shot is heard off stage and Dorn informs Trigorin – and us – that Trepliov has killed himself.

So, a gunshot and a death – the same scenario as marked the conclusion of *Hedda Gabler*. But whereas Hedda Gabler is at the centre of Ibsen's play Trepliov is not at the centre of Chekhov's. Fundamentally *The Seagull* is an ensemble piece with the seagull Nina having the strongest claim for being the central character. Does this therefore disqualify *The Seagull* from being viewed as a tragedy? Chekhov himself certainly saw his plays as basically comedies and disliked the tragic emphasis that Stanislavsky put on them. For example on *The Cherry Orchard*, on which he dyingly[6] struggled to write four lines a day, Chekhov commented that it was "not a drama but a comedy: in places almost a farce." And whereas the directors, Stanislavsky and Nemirov-Danchenko (the co-director too of *The Seagull* who had taken the decision not to accede to Chekhov's sister's request not to go ahead with performing *The Seagull* at the Moscow Art Theatre) saw *The Cherry Orchard* as "a serious drama of Russian life" Chekhov continued to see it as "a light comedy." I just think that on this subject Chekhov is wrong. He did, after all, acknowledge, when commenting on his play *The Three Sisters*: "The play turned out to be dreary, long, and awkward: I say awkward because it has, for instance, four heroines and a spirit more gloomy than gloom itself." We need, as always, to trust the play, not the playwright.

In a way this is all an academic discussion. We do not need to fit plays into strait-jacketed categories in accordance with Aristotle or anyone else's definitions of tragedy. Chekhov's plays continue to resonate as they comment on the misery of individuals and the collapse of the society they have known. Trepliov kills himself; Nina goes off to act in provincial theatre, being treated as little more than a whore; Arkadina clings on to her beauty and her money as her career fades; Masha marries, without love, a boring schoolteacher; Sorin is dying, completely unfulfilled and lonely; even the apparently successful Trigorin sees life as fatuous and admits to Nina that "I've never liked myself. I dislike myself as a writer." Misery, unhappiness everywhere.

Look at the unhappiness in love too. Masha loves Trepliov who loves Nina who loves Trigorin who loves Arkadina. Arkadina loves only herself. Nowhere is love reciprocated.

And everybody is lonely. Not the stuff of comedy.

Chekhov did not want his characters to be larger than life or archetypes, as I have argued; he specifically did not wish to "put them on stilts." Writing *Ivanov* he commented: "Let the things that happen on the stage be as complex and yet just as simple as they are in life. For instance, people are having a meal at the table, just having a meal, but at the same time their happiness is being created, or their lives are being smashed up." Obviously it is the smashing up rather than the creation of any happiness that permeates Chekhov's plays. Maxim Gorky got it right when he wrote: "No one understood so clearly as Anton Chekhov the tragic elements of life's trivialities; before him no one was able to convey to people, with such ruthless truthfulness, the shamefulness and boredom of their life in all its monotony and dreariness."

Individual misery runs through *The Seagull*. In this play it is stronger than the theme of the collapse of society. Although with Sorin dying and his nephew Trepliov dead and Madam Arkadina needing society life and hating being in the country, what will happen to the family estate is clearly in question – and we get a clue when the bailiff, managing the estate, has his way over the use of horses at the expense of Arkadina's wishes. But it is in Chekhov's last play *The Cherry Orchard* that we find the strongest expression of the collapse of contemporary Russian society and of the aristocracy in particular.

Chekhov's childhood involved the mismanagement of his mother's property: she was cheated by an apparent friend and builders, and his childhood home in Taganrog had to be sold off. In later life, returning to Taganrog, he was horrified by the deforestation that had taken place. He was in love too with cherry orchards from his childhood, and in adulthood planted a cherry orchard on his own country estate – and the bulk of this orchard was destroyed by the man he later sold it to. In *The Cherry Orchard* Madame Raneskaya presides over an estate which has become financially unviable[7]. She herself has no understanding of financial matters, so when suggestions are made that, in order to save the estate a portion of it, including the nationally renowned cherry orchard, should be sold for the purposes of building summer cottages, she ignores them and continues to give away money that she cannot afford. She is drifting incompetently through life, ignoring the tumbrils at her door. Of course all the individual characters are unfulfilled and therefore dissatisfied. The play ends with the family leaving their estate, which has been sold to Lopakhin, the son of a former serf, and to the sound of axes cutting down the cherry orchard. Firs, the 87-year-old eccentric servant, who has served the family all his life is callously forgotten about and left behind to die – and his death ends the play!

A society that is falling apart, full of individual unhappiness and blind to the realities of the present – those are Chekhov's themes. True they are full of wry comedy and Chekhov laughs (but not cruelly) at his characters; indeed, as he said in his letters, he was non-judgmental. He was presenting society as he saw it. And there is depth and complexity in his characters, an unspoken subtext prevails. Ivanov's comment in the play of the same name that "…we all have too many wheels, and screws, and valves inside us to be judged by first impressions or by a few external traits, I don't understand you, you don't understand me, and we don't understand ourselves" is most apt.

So Chekhov has created a wonderful portrait gallery of people who don't understand themselves or the direction in which society is moving. In *The Seagull* only Trepliov and Nina refuse to accept the world of the past: one of them commits suicide, the other, through experience, comes to believe that "endurance" is what really matters. Hope dies, and for everyone it is not an option. It is all a tragic twilight world of disillusion and failure. And no one creates such a world better than Chekhov.

---

1 This was a successful reworking of his earlier failed play *The Wood Demon* (1889).

2 Tolstoy's *Tsar Fiodor Ivanovich*.

3 Shakespeare's *The Merchant of Venice*.

4 She was to become Chekhov's wife – he had fallen in love with her playing the role of Irina in Tolstoy's *Tsar Fiodor Ivanovich*.

5 Nina is the most interesting character in the play. Carey Mulligan, who played her at the Royal Court in 2007, described her as "the ultimate female role." I regret that I did not see this production: David Hare described Carey Mulligan's performance as the most convincing of then twenty-four productions he had seen of *The Seagull*.

6 He died some four and a half month's later, his last drink being a glass of champagne given him by his doctor.

7 The serfs in Russia had been emancipated under Tsar Alexander II in 1861, roughly 21 million of them. This left 50,000 landlords of estates more than 110 hectares in difficulties about finding the money to pay for labour.

GEORGE BERNARD SHAW: *Saint Joan*

Joan of Arc[1] is the most renowned woman in French history. She has appeared on French stamps in 1929, 1946, 1968, 1979, 1996 and 2012. Not just in Rheims where she crowned the Dauphin, but in the Place des Pyramides in Paris and throughout France[2] we find statues of this remarkable nineteen-year-old young woman who was canonised as late as the 16th May 1920, nearly five hundred years after she was burnt at the stake for heresy, witchcraft and sorcery. But her reputation is worldwide and she remains a figurehead and symbol in universal consciousness. In the world of music, Verdi and Tchaikovsky wrote operas about her; in modern times Leonard Cohen wrote a memorable song about her in his *Songs of Love and Hate* album of 1970, Elton John and Bernie Taupin in 2002, Kate Bush in her *Aerial* album of 2005 and Katy Perry in her 2010 *Teenage Dream* album, all reference her. I am told that she also features in a number of video games. She has captured the public imagination for all time.

In the world of poetry Voltaire wrote a mock heroic poem, *The Maid of Oranges* in 1756, pretty ruthlessly debunking the Joan myth, and the English Poet Laureate Robert Southey also published an epic poem *Joan of Arc* in 1796. The best novel – infrequently read but regarded by its author as his finest work – is Mark Twain's *Personal Recollections of Joan of Arc*, researched for months in France and published under the name of Jean Francois Alden. There are other novels too, most notably Thomas Keneally's *Blood Red, Sister Rose* – and she is referenced by Terry Pratchett in his *Monstrous Regiment*. It is in the world of theatre, though, that Joan's story predominates. I will mention only the most well-known plays. There is Shakespeare's *Henry VI Part 1* in which she is portrayed as a cunning, evil witch; there is Schiller's *The Maid of Orleans*, a Romantic response to Voltaire's viewpoint which is said to have spawned over eighty plays about Joan in the nineteenth century; there is Brecht's *Saint Joan of the Stockyards*, where she is portrayed as a labour leader in Chicago; and there is Anouilh's *L'Alouette (The*

Lark) which limits itself to the trial, verdict and execution of Joan, drawing parallels both with the French Vichy regime and with McCarthyism in the United States – and is translated by Lillian Hellman, with music by Leonard Bernstein. Films of Joan of Arc have not usually been successful: Ingrid Bergman, directed by Victor Fleming in 1948 and Jean Seberg, directed by Otto Preminger in 1957 – the later scripted by Graham Greene from Shaw's play – both starred, with limited distinction, as Joan.

Shaw's *Saint Joan* was first performed on Broadway on the 28th December 1923. The text was published in 1924 and on the 26th March of that year was performed in London, with Sybil Thorndike playing, as Shaw had envisaged, Joan. (It is a coveted role for actresses, and has been played by, amongst others, Wendy Hiller, Siobhan McKenna, Joan Plowright, Genevieve Bujold, Lynn Redgrave, Imelda Staunton, Frances de la Tour and – most recently at The National Theatre – by Ann-Marie Duff.) Shaw had studied closely the records of the trial and 26.5% of the play centres on the trial, the rest is from Shaw's imagination. He has tried, though, to be fair-minded to Joan, refusing to go down the path taken by Shakespeare (he actually suspects that Shakespeare had little to do with *Henry VI Part 1)*, and writing that "Schiller's Joan has not a single point of contact with the real Joan" and that Twain had been "converted to downright worship of Joan."

These latter remarks are taken from a lengthy Preface to the play. Shaw was fond of his Prefaces and expressed the opinion that he wished Shakespeare had written just one Preface rather than ten of his plays! But this is mainly part of Shaw's self-aggrandisement, a part of which is comparing himself with Shakespeare and finding himself superior. This comparison between the two "Sh's" that he is fond of making is partly to arouse attention to new, contemporary drama as opposed to "a veneration of old masters" – and he does admit that "no man will ever write a better tragedy than Lear" – but it is only partly so. We find Shaw writing: "With the single exception of Homer, there is no eminent writer, not even Sir Walter Scott[3], whom I can despise so entirely as I despise Shakespeare when I measure my mind against his." To be fair to Shaw he **was** concerned with the contemporary theatre and how it could confront hypocrisy and problems in society and to this end he wrote a long essay on *The Quintessence of Ibsenism* (1891) extolling the virtues and relevance of Ibsen's plays – though, again it is often Shaw who is being written about rather than Ibsen!

In Shaw's *Saint Joan* we first meet Joan persuading Robert de Baudricourt to lend her some of his men and finance a horse and man's armour for her so that she can lift the siege of Orleans. In asking this she is following the instructions of her "voices", that is Saints Margaret and Catherine and the archangel Michael. Having initially refused to see Joan forty-eight hours previously, de Baudricourt agrees to see this 17 to 18-year-old girl who is "always talking to soldiers." She spells out to him that it is God's will that the English, who are besieging and close to capturing Orleans, should stay in their own country, England, and that after she has defeated them at Orleans she should crown the Dauphin King of France in Rheims Cathedral. Finally won over by Joan's arguments and confidence – "there is something about her" – he accedes to her requests and she departs for Orleans. What also happens is that de Baudricourt's "three barbary hens and the black one" now start laying eggs, something they had not done since Joan's arrival at then castle of Vaucouleurs, prompting the last words of the scene from de Baudricourt: "Christ in heaven! She did come from God."

In the second scene the Dauphin is presented as "a poor creature physically" with "a cheeky humour." The Archbishop of Rheims, believing it important that the Church examines "the girl", grants permission for Joan to be brought before the Dauphin and his court. Gilles de Rais, "Bluebeard", pretends to be the Dauphin, but Joan is not fooled. The Dauphin admits that he is afraid and scarcely has the strength to lift a sword: "I am quiet and sensible; and I don't want to kill people." But he is emboldened by Joan and he gives command of the army to The Maid. Captain La Hire, a "war dog", who early in the scene had pronounced Joan "an angel dressed as a soldier", impressed by the way she had made the tortuous journey from Vaucouleurs to Rheims through enemy forces without encountering any difficulties, concludes the scene, drawing his sword and proclaiming "For God and His Maid! To Orleans!"

The third scene takes place some fifty-two days later by the banks of the Loire outside Orleans. Dunois, known as the Bastard of

Orleans and in charge of the king's army, has been waiting for the wind to change direction so that his troops can cross the river and attack the encamped English from the rear. Joan arrives, belligerently wishing to lead the army across the bridge. Dunois explains that that is tactically suicidal and that not a soldier will follow her. He persuades her that they have to wait for a change of wind, and even as she sets off for the nearest church to pray to Saint Catherine for a west wind, the wind changes to the propitious, wanted direction. "God has spoken," says Dunois, and kneels and hands over his baton to Joan, giving her control of the king's army.

At the beginning of the fourth scene we learn that Joan has defeated the English armies not only at Orleans, but also at Jargeau, Meung, Beaugency and Patay. The situation is seen from the perspective of the English army, and various discussions reveal the different aspects of opposition to Joan: the English chaplain sees her as a witch because "no Englishman is ever fairly beaten"; more seriously a nobleman, the Earl of Warwick, deplores how nationality as a concept is gaining acceptance, which will mean the loss of authority of feudal lords and of the Church; the Bishop of Beauvais, Peter Cauchon, believes neither in Joan's witchcraft nor her miracles, but for him she is a heretic, acting "as if she herself were The Church." Cauchon also deplores her Nationalism "for the Catholic Church knows only one realm, and that is the realm of Christ's kingdom." Warwick and the chaplain, John de Stogumber, clearly want to burn Joan, whereas Cauchon's priority is "to strive to the utmost for this woman's salvation."

Scene Five opens with Joan kneeling in prayer in the cathedral of Rheims. She has crowned the Dauphin King but she is not popular at court and sees only Dunois as a friend. Joan is talking of going back to her home in Domremy once she has relieved the siege of Compiegne and then taken Paris. But the Archbishop sees that Joan is no longer clothed with humility but rather exemplifies hubris. The new King, Charles VII, petulantly thinks Joan's voices should speak to him. Even Dunois points out that generalship was important in their military successes. Bluebeard sums up the thoughts of most of the court: "Not content with being Pope Joan, you must be Caesar and Alexander as well." Joan has little support at court, but still believing in the godliness of her voices, she storms off to relieve the siege of Compiegne, where, we learn at the beginning of Scene VI, without adequate military support, she is captured by the Burgundians.

It is now nine months later. The Earl of Warwick bought Joan for an undisclosed "very handsome sum" (before Compiegne he had offered £16,000 for her capture) five months after her capture, and three months ago he handed her across to the Bishop of Beauvais for her to be tried for heresy. Warwick is impatient for a result but the Church is determined that Joan shall have a fair trial. The Inquisitor asserts: "The heretic in the hands of the Holy Office is safe from violence, is assured of a fair trial, and cannot suffer death, even when guilty, if repentance follows sin." Cauchon talks of the Church being betrayed from within by the "arch heresy... of Protestantism." Under examination Joan insists that God, through her voices, speaks directly to her; she continues to resist the authority of the Church and is threatened with excommunication and burning at the stake. At last confronted with this real consequence of her voices she recants and makes her mark, signing her confession. But then she learns that she will be "shut from the light of the sky and the sight of the fields and flowers" for ever as she is sentenced to "perpetual imprisonment." She withdraws her confession, is formally excommunicated and the English soldiers rush her out – with the Inquisitor acknowledging that she was "a young and innocent creature" – to be burned at the awaiting stake. We learn of the impact of her death: she had warned Brother Martin Ladvenu to look to his own safety as he held a cross before her burning self and he believed that her Saviour appeared to her and that "this is not the end for her but the beginning"; the English chaplain who had been most clamorous in demanding Joan's death has been moved to see her as now in Jesus' bosom and himself likely to be damned to all eternity; and the executioner tells us that "her heart would not burn."

The Epilogue is a fantasy scene some twenty-five years later. Warwick's doubts, the last words of Scene VI, that we had seen the last of Joan, are realised. King Charles VII is in bed and is visited by various figures from Joan's past. First of all Brother Martin Ladvenu informs us that "the sentence on her is broken, annulled, annihilated, set aside as non-existent, without value or effect" and that "her judges were full of corruption, cozenage, fraud, and malice." Which he (and we) know to be "four falsehoods." Joan then appears, as do: Cauchon; Dunois; an English soldier who, because he "tied two sticks together, and gave them to a poor lass who was going to be burned" has a day off from hell every year; the English chaplain de Stogumber; the Executioner; the Earl of Warwick; the Archbishop; and the Inquisitor. Finally a gentleman dressed in the fashion of 1920 appears to much amusement, but he is there to declare that the Church now "calls the said Venerable and Blessed Joan to the communion of the Church Triumphant as Saint Joan." All her visitors, and Charles, then kneel before her and praise her individually, but when Joan threatens to return from the dead, they all make excuses and leave. Cauchon has already uttered the memorable words: "Must then a Christ perish in torment in every age to save those who have no imagination" and the play's final words are with Joan: "O God that madest this beautiful earth, when will it be ready to receive Thy saints? How long, O Lord, how long?"

That is quite a chunk of narrative, but it has involved bringing out the relevant issues: for Shaw it is the issues – as Tony Benn used to say – that are important. In his lengthy Preface he discusses forty-one aspects of the life, times and trial of Joan of Arc and then dramatises the salient points for discussion in the play. Points such as her voices, nationalism, the power of the church, her "miracles", her dressing as a soldier, Protestantism, her immaturity and ignorance, the fairness of the trial and so on. Shaw is offering evidence, filtered through his own acerbic mind, for discussion.

In the course of doing so, he resorts to cheap humour and melodrama. The hens laying at the end of the first Scene for example as a proof that Joan came from God simply elicits disbelieving laughter. Shaw's portrayal of the English chaplain, John de Stogumber, as a buffoon, claiming that God spoke only in English and then his melodramatic conversion to believing in the holiness of Joan are not only laughable but close to risible. I think it fair to say that his characters are one dimensional, representing one perspective only. "There are no villains in this piece," writes Shaw. He sees villains as a playwright's mechanical contrivances and likely to make Joan less interesting.[4] He may be right but it is usually the tension between complex characters that makes for good drama. Shaw settles for tension between ideas.

So, can we actually classify *Saint Joan* as a tragedy? Everything centres round Joan herself. She fulfils the requirements of a tragic heroine's fall from a great height: she has successfully led the French army and crowned the Dauphin King and then been burned, initially ignominiously, at the stake by the English who insisted on seeing her as a witch. Only briefly does she struggle against the script that has been written for her, or fate, and it can be argued that she writes her own script anyway. Hearing voices and being propelled into action by those voices – do they come from within or from without? And can her voices speak to her as simply as through the rhythm of church bells? Dunois points out the obvious: "we shall hear whatever we fancy in the booming of the bell." Defensively, responding to an angry Archbishop, Joan does admit the possibility of the voices being "only the echoes of my own commonsense."

Clearly this last quotation is what the rationalist Shaw believes: he puts all visionary experiences down to a vivid imagination. Similarly with regard to miracles, Shaw has the Archbishop say that miracles "are often very simple and innocent contrivances by which the priest fortifies the faith of his flock." They may appear wonderful to witnesses and simple to those who perform them; "that does not matter: if they confirm or create faith they are true miracles." Shaw rationalising again.

But I digress. And that is one of Shaw's undoubted strengths: he sets you off on a chase after his ideas. The question to consider is the tragic hero status of Joan of Arc. It could be argued that she is completely in control of her own fate, that she wills, almost in a suicidal manner her own death. (She does say that she was going to return to the country just a year after her military successes began – and yet her capture at Compiegne is sixteen months after the relief of the siege of Orleans.) She is not playing an unexpected part in a drama that the gods are working through; she is scarcely torn between two conflicting moral demands. There is merely a brief moment of vacillation when she recants, only to find that imprisonment for life is what is then on offer, causing a volte-face to her original position – "your counsel is of the devil… mine is of God."

So the purists may be unhappy at calling *St Joan* a tragedy. Shaw's discussion on whether the play is a tragedy or a melodrama in his Preface is singularly unhelpful. But I think that what matters is that the play – eventually – works on stage and that we feel for the spiritually innocent (child of God?) and shed cathartic tears both at her burning and at her final rejection in the Epilogue. I began this essay by writing of Joan's impact as a symbol in different aspects of culture. And why I think this is so is that, not only does she appeal to the patriot and the protestant, she is also a rock-solid anti-establishment figure[5]. She defied the feudal lords and the church, spitting (with the apparent blessing of God) in the face of well-heeled, self-righteous authority. Manifestly energising and charismatic too, the world is always in need of heroines like Joan of Arc.

(A footnote. Shaw wrote over fifty plays. He was sixty-seven when he wrote *Saint Joan*. Most of his plays that are still performed were written before *Saint Joan*: the only post *Saint Joan* plays that can occasionally be seen are *The Apple Cart* (1929) and *Too Good to be True* (1932). He was awarded the Nobel Prize for Literature in 1925, not insignificantly I think, shortly after *Saint Joan* was written and produced.)

---

[1] She never used the name Joan of Arc: she was Jeanne la Pucelle – "Joan the Maid."

[2] Not only in France. In the United States there are statues of Joan in Washington D.C., New Orleans and Philadelphia for example.

[3] Shaw preferred Scott's *Rob Roy* to Shakespeare's *Macbeth*…

[4] Shaw is in fact pushing his own social agenda – that righteous, innocent people commit most murder. This is a view which is increasingly gaining credence.

[5] Joan was a poster girl for the suffragettes, promoting the Suffragette newspaper. And when, in 1909, the Women's Social and Political Union marched through London, they were led by an armour-clad horse-riding "Joan."

EUGENE O'NEILL:
Mourning Becomes Electra

Eugene O'Neill was born in a hotel (now a Starbuck's) in what is now Times Square in 1888. The birth is commemorated with a plaque, declaring: "Eugene O'Neill ...America's greatest playwright was born on this site." It is distinctly debatable whether he is America's greatest playwright – Arthur Miller and Tennessee Williams have formidable claims to that accolade – but there is no questioning his prolificity: thirty-two full length plays were written between 1914 and 1933 and twenty or more one-act plays were written in the 1910s. It is, of course, his full-length plays with which we are concerned and the choice is not straightforward: he won four Pulitzer prizes – for *Beyond the Horizon* in 1920, *Anna Christie* in 1922, *Strange Interlude* in 1928 and *Long Day's Journey into Night* in 1957. In addition, during a period of twelve years from 1934 to 1946 when O'Neill produced no more plays, he was awarded the Nobel Prize for Literature in 1936.

I have chosen not to write about any of the above four plays, but each warrants a few words so at least the range of O'Neill's themes and skills can begin to be appreciated. *Beyond the Horizon* tells the story of two brothers, Robert and Andrew, who both love the same girl, Ruth. Ruth marries Robert who stays to mange the family farm while Andrew goes off to sea. Ruth realises four months into her marriage that she has married the wrong brother. They get into debt, lose a child and Robert contracts tuberculosis. It's an emotionally complex wrangle, yet the brothers clearly love each other. (*Desire under the Elms* (1924) is also set on a farm and similarly there are two men fighting over the same woman, Abbie, but this time it is father and stepson and it involves deep passions and infanticide. Deliberately O'Neill is echoing the Greek myth of Phaedra, Theseus and Hippolytus.)

Anna Christie is initially set in a bar in New York where a father, Old Chris, meets up with his daughter that he has not seen since she was five. She agrees to go and live/work on his barge with him and the next three Acts are set on the barge. It transpires that she had been raped as a child and had worked as a prostitute. This requires some adjustment from her father and a stoker, Mat, who loves her. In the end there is both redemption and forgiveness, which also sees Anna forgiving her father for abandoning her all those years ago.

The story of *Strange Interlude* is yet again about love and sex. Nina loses her fiancé in the First World War. The relationship had not been consummated and, on learning of his death, she sets about sleeping around. Eventually she marries an affable if uninspiring man called Sam Evans, and becomes pregnant by him. Then she learns that insanity runs in the family, so Nina aborts Sam's child and quickly conceives another child with Ned Darell. Sam know nothing of this, and believes her child to be his. Unfortunately Nina and Ned fall in love... And Gordon Evans, coming to manhood, believes Sam is his father. It is a more than intense family drama; it was seen at the time to contain "adult content" and as such it was banned in certain US states. It's a long play, as is actually the wont with O'Neill, and stylistically is interesting for his experiment with stream of consciousness thought and soliloquy, with the actors addressing the audience and revealing, usually briefly through asides, their real, innermost thinking.

Long Day's Journey into Night is the most obviously autobiographical of O'Neill's plays. Again we have a dysfunctional family: the father and his two sons are alcoholics and the mother is a morphine addict. The father, James, is an actor who has toured in one role for years and has been so associated with that role that other opportunities, especially Shakespearean ones, have been denied him; he is financially secure, through property investment but short of day-to-day cash, and at 65 is resentful of his handling of his life. He turns a blind eye to his wife's morphine habit. When the play opens she, Mary, has returned from a clinic for morphine addiction, but it is clear that, throughout *Long Day's Journey into Night* she remains drug dependent. A Catholic Irish woman she spells out her unhappiness in Act Three of the play when she wishes that one day she would accidentally overdose and die – something she cannot do on purpose as the Virgin Mary would never forgive her. The elder son, Jamie, is a womaniser and an alcoholic, but, like his father, finds it difficult to get work as an actor owing to his innate irresponsibility. The younger brother, Edmund, has worked in the merchant navy and in doing so has caught tuberculosis. It is a sick family, and as well as their dramatic interactions we learn that James's father emigrated to the States from Ireland when James was eight, abandoned his family and returned to Ireland two years later and died of taking rat poison. We learn too that a pre-marriage affair of James's so shocked Mary's friends that they shunned her. And, amongst a good deal more, we learn that James and Mary's second son Eugene had died of measles at the age of two, infected by Jamie, probably deliberately. Oh, and Mary's father had died of tuberculosis!

The play's four Acts all take place on the same day, from 8.30 in the morning to midnight: the title of the play is totally apt. It is set in 1912 and the characters in *Long Day's Journey into Night* correspond to the exact age of O'Neill's parents and himself and his sibling Jamie. The Christian names of O'Neill's parents are retained in the play and there is a simple swap round between the names Edmund and Eugene. Moreover O'Neill's father was an actor who played the part of the Count of Monte Cristo some six hundred times; his mother like her namesake in the play did attend a Catholic school in the Midwest; his elder brother Jamie did drink himself to death; and Eugene himself suffered from alcoholism and depression **and** tuberculosis – indeed it was only after his time in a tuberculosis sanatorium the O'Neill focused on writing plays, prior to that his having enjoyed sailing around the world in merchant ships.

Autobiographically, then, O'Neill had experienced much of the fraught family situations that he explores in so many of his plays. Briefly, I want to add that O'Neill's relationships with his wives and children were far from text-book ideal: his first marriage lasted three years and produced one son, Eugene O'Neill, Jr; his second marriage lasted eleven years and produced two children, Shane and Oona; within a month of leaving his wife and children, he then married, for the third and last time, the actress Carlotta Monterey. In later life Monterey became addicted to potassium bromide, but it is his relationship with his children to which I want to draw attention. When in 1943, aged 18, his daughter Oona married the fifty-four year old Charlie Chaplin he promptly disowned her and never saw her again during the remaining ten years of his life. Eugene O'Neill, Jr was an alcoholic and committed suicide at the age of forty in 1950. And his other son, Shane, became a heroine addict, was disowned by his father and too committed suicide – by jumping out of a window.

So when we look at O'Neill's plays – and especially *Mourning Becomes Electra* – and we see the cruelty and pain of family interaction, we know that O'Neill is writing from experience. There is no pussy-footing around with tentative abstract exploration of a theme which might be intellectually interesting. O'Neill grabs us by the throat and demands our attention. His flesh and blood characters are not averse to revealing, without prompting, their love and hate for each other – and in *Mourning Becomes Electra* these passions are all kept within the family, daughter to father, brother to mother, mother to daughter, father to son.

It is this Freudian incest theme which is mainly why I have chosen to more fully explore *Mourning Becomes Electra*. That together with the attractively poetic title (O'Neill is expert at alluring titles) and, especially, its deliberate links with Greek drama. What O'Neill is doing in this play is writing a twentieth-century version of Aeschylus' *Oresteia*. He even makes links between the names of characters: Agamemnon becomes General Mannon; Orestes becomes Orin and so on. Not at all subtle. But O'Neill does embrace the whole Greek tragic concept: there is a group of occasional bystanders who serve as a kind of Chorus; the Mannon family is seen as a doomed family expiating its past; fate and free will are therefore issues; the house outside and within which most of the action takes place has columns and is in the style of a Greek temple; O'Neill tells us that all four of the main protagonists have a "lifelike mask quality"[1]. All these matters will be discussed later, but for now it is time to get to grips with the story.

Mourning Becomes Electra is in fact a trilogy: *The Homecoming*, *The Hunted*, and *The Haunted*. So producing all three plays, preferably on the same day, and preferably without a break, is a mammoth task for actors and audience: even with some cutting Howard Davies' production for the National Theatre in 2003, with Helen Mirren, Eve Best and Tim Piggott-Smith lasted four and a half hours.

The Homecoming begins with the anticipated arrival of Brigadier-General Ezra Mannon from the American Civil War. His daughter Lavinia eagerly awaits his return. She confesses that she can never marry anyone because her father "needs her." Her faithful friend Peter has proposed marriage to her and she has also been courted by a Captain Adam Brant. Brant appears and he discloses that his father was Ezra Mannon's brother and his mother a socially inferior Canuck nurse, and that this irregular liaison had meant his father's expulsion from the family. Brant has vowed revenge. In Act Two we learn that Christine, Lavinia's mother, is having an affair with Brant, his flirtation with Lavinia (or Vinnie) being simply a smokescreen. Christine admits that she hates her husband and sees Vinnie as his child whereas her son Orin is hers alone to love. Christine appears to accept Lavinia's demand that she never sees Brant again, but later agrees that she and Brant poison Ezra on his return and attribute his death to the heart trouble that she, Lavinia[2], has been at pains to exaggerate.

Act Three marks the actual homecoming. Ironically Ezra has realised how loveless has been his marriage – "there's always been some barrier between us" – and he wants now "to smash down" that barrier. He admits that he "turned to Vinnie. But a daughter's not a wife." Vinnie has drawn her father's attention to her mother and Brant, but Christine reassures her husband that nothing is going on and indeed, calculatingly, says: "There is no wall between us. I love you."

"Father, how can you love that shameless harlot," shouts Vinnie at the shuttered window of her parents' bedroom.

Although she "has given herself" that night and let her husband "take her like a nigger slave …bought at auction", Christine sneaks out of her husband's bed early in the morning in Act Four. Christine no longer keeps up a pretence and taunts her husband with her being Brant's mistress and Brant being the son of the Nanuck nurse, Marie Brantome. Mannon, irate almost beyond words, threatens to kill her but falls, clutching his heart and calls for medicine. Christine puts a pellet on his tongue, and Ezra's last words are: "Help, Vinnie …She's guilty …not medicine." *The Homecoming* ends with Vinnie promising that her mother will pay for the crime she has committed.

There are five Acts in *The Hunted*. In Act One Orin returns, initially disappointed not to find his mother waiting for him. He questions Vinnie about his mother and Brant and Vinnie continues to remind her brother of Christine's behaviour. There is, though, a loving reunion between Orin and his mother – "My boy! My baby!" – and the short Act ends with Christine trying to justify to Vinnie her relationship with Brant, partly in terms of her fidelity to her husband for the previous twenty-three years. In Act Two Christine and Vinnie battle for Orin's mind: "I'm convinced she's actually insane," says Christine of Vinnie. Sitting at his mother's feet Orin recounts the escapist dream he had of the two of them together in the South Sea Islands, where there was "peace and warmth and security." The idyll is broken by Vinnie insisting that Orin comes to see their father's body, and Christine realises that she has to warn Brant of the fury and jealousy that might be enacted upon him. In Act Three Vinnie has difficulty in convincing her brother that their mother has a lover and he eventually agrees that he will believe her "when you find them together."

Act Four of *The Hunted* is mainly set on Brant's clipper ship, two days after Mannon's funeral. Christine and Brant are talking in the cabin below, and Vinnie and Orin are on the deck above, listening in. Christine and Brant are arranging to sail away on the ship *Atlantis* on Friday morning, sailing to the Blessed Isles where Brant hopes that they "can still find happiness and forget." Orin is horrified that it is **his** island and **his** dream she is talking about and it is with Brant that she wishes to go and not himself. So, after Christine has left, Orin shoots Brant at point-blank range and they trash the cabin and ransack his pockets to give the appearance of a burglary. In death, though, Brant resembles Mannon; it seems to Orin that he has killed his father. Orin's penultimate speech in Act Four as he stares at the body of Brant is: "If I had been he I would have done what he did! I would have loved her as he loved her – and killed father too – for her sake!" Act Five is brief. Almost gleefully Orin tells his mother of the murder of Brant, and Christine collapses. He then promises to make his mother forget "that servant's bastard ... that low swine" Brant and proposes: "I'll make you happy! We'll leave Vinnie here and go away on a long voyage – to the South Seas –". Christine, however goes into her husband's study and shoots herself with his pistol. Orin thinks he drove her to it and that he is responsible for her death, but Vinnie promises him that "I'll love you. I'll help you to forget" and gives orders to Seth Beckwith, the Mannons' seventy-five year old gardener and man of all work to go for the doctor: "Tell him Mother has killed herself in a fit of insane grief over Father's death."

It is a year later when *The Haunted* begins. Vinnie and Orin are back from a voyage to China and Vinnie expresses the hope that "The dead have forgotten us! We've forgotten them!" What is apparent, though, is that Vinnie now, almost perfectly, resembles her mother and Orin his father. There are two other characters in *The Haunted* who, though present in the other two plays, now assume an importance in this play: Peter and Hazel, brother and sister, who each has a potential marriage relationship with the Mannon children, Vinnie and Orin respectively. At the start of the second Scene in the First Act Orin laments: "Love! – What right have I – or you – to love?" "Every right!" replies Vinnie defiantly. And his mother now encourages Peter's affections. It appears that Vinnie and Orin had spent time on the Islands, which Orin jokes as being "Vinnie's islands" because she fell in love with the Islanders. Vinnie found peace and the beauty of love, witnessing the sinless life of the islanders, and proposes marriage to a delighted Peter. "I want to be rid of the past," she says, so does not want the increasingly cynical and morbid Orin to live with them. Act Two is a month later and Orin, in his father's study, is writing a family history, beginning with the crimes of their Grandfather Abe down to the present day crimes: he finds Vinnie "the most interesting criminal of us all!" In Orin's eyes his sister is now, like their mother, looking with desire at men and has even bought clothes in the colours that their mother wore. He has become engaged to Hazel but sees himself in the role of his father and his sister in the role of her mother. He will not permit Vinnie to leave him and marry Peter: "I'm the Mannon you're chained to!" he insists. And, fearful of either being killed by or left by Vinnie, he is going to put the family history, "the confession", into Hazel's hands.

In Act Three Orin pleads to Hazel "For God's sake, Hazel, if you love me help me to get away from here – or something terrible will happen!" He hands Hazel the big sealed envelope, the family history, entreating her to open it only if something happens to him or the day before Vinnie and Peter are due to wed: Vinnie must not have happiness – she's got to be punished. And Hazel must not love him any more, for he loves Vinnie. Vinnie sees the sealed envelope which Hazel is hiding and demands it. Desperately Vinnie tells her brother: "You know I love you! Make Hazel give that up and I'll do anything you want me to!" This is enough for Orin to take back the envelope for it also gives him power over his sister and he insists that she must never see Peter again. Orin is by now all over the place emotionally: he lovingly strokes his sister's hair, he talks of confessing their crimes and finding peace together, he talks of Death being an Island of Peace and reuniting with his mother. For Vinnie, of course, there is nothing to confess: what they did was "only justice." But, burdened with guilt, Orin goes into his father's study and shoots himself.

Neither Seth nor Hazel believe the story that Orin accidentally killed himself while cleaning his pistol, and Seth encourages Vinnie to marry Peter and "git clear" for "there's no rest in this house which Grandfather built as a temple of Hate and Death." Vinnie throws herself into Peter's arms and demands an immediate marriage, and in doing so, says "Want me! Take me, Adam!" She realises there really is no escape from the past: "Always the dead between! ...Love isn't permitted to me. The dead are too strong!" And she pivots sharply on her heel and marches into the Mannon house, shutting the door behind her, vowing never to go out again. "I'm the last Mannon. I've got to punish myself! ...It takes the Mannons to punish themselves for being born!"

I hope that lengthy narrative of the trilogy presents clearly what O'Neill's themes and main concerns are. I will, though, spell them out once again. There is the apparent doom or curse on the house of Mannon. When Vinnie shuts herself into the Greek-templed Mannon house she is going to be daily reminded of the family fate, as the portraits of the Mannon family, alarmingly similar, are everywhere, oppressively looking down on her. We know that the Mannon's have been "top dog" in the community for "near on two hundred years"; we know that Grandfather Mannon had too lusted after the Canuck nurse and had consequently disowned his son David (who, incidentally, was a drunken wife-beater). *Mourning*

Becomes Electra then follows the murderous and suicidal destruction of The Mannon family. Only with Vinnie's death will the curse be finished. It resembles truly Greek tragedy – not the House of Atreus but the House of Mannon.[3]

It is all very explicitly Freudian too. There is some loose use of the word "love", but it is clear that Vinnie unhealthily loves her father, that Orin unhealthily loves his mother, that Orin unhealthily is attracted to his sister. Sex or the possibilities of sexual liaisons is everywhere. To some extent the way O'Neill crudely presents the Oedipus and Electra complexes is close to laughable: subtle it is not.

Which leads me on to a very real criticism of O'Neill: everything is trowelled on. From the beginning he sets about hitting the audience with a sledgehammer and never relents. (I was conscious when typing out quotations from the plays that almost every single line ended with an exclamation mark.) Arguably, therefore, we have melodrama rather than drama. It could be questioned too that there is no central tragic figure – though a similar criticism could be levelled at Aeschylus' trilogy. With Electra, though, at least we have a central sympathetic character. In *Mourning Becomes Electra* no one, certainly not Vinnie, is sympathetic. Warmth, justice and morality all seem absent from the play.[4] It is as though O'Neill has started with a template for a sexually dysfunctional family, à la Freud, and then, humourlessly, pushed this concept to its dramatic limits. It has to be conceded, though, that in the course of doing so he has grabbed and not let go of the audience's attention – and has written two superb female parts.

There is more to be said about the achievements of O'Neill too. Between the Wars he brought seriousness and style to the American theatre, qualities that had previously been associated with European imports like Ibsen, Chekhov and Shaw. He immersed himself in the whole tradition of theatre from Aeschylus onwards and experimented with Noh theatre and verse drama; he was a serious playwright with a prodigious output. He was capable of self-criticism: after the successful 1932 production of *Mourning Becomes Electra* he wrote: "It needed great language to lift it beyond itself. I haven't got that." But he did have an ear for contemporary American idiom, creating plausible dialogue (sometimes masking the incredibility of plot), and perhaps we should leave the last word with his fellow Nobel Literature laureate (1930), Sinclair Lewis, who wrote of O'Neill: "Eugene O'Neill ... has done nothing much in the American drama save to transform it utterly ... from a false world of neat and competent trickery to a world of splendour, fear and greatness." Eugene O'Neill, a playwright of importance.

---

[1] Referencing the mask worn by all actors in classical Greek theatre.

[2] I shall refer to her as Vinnie from now on.

[3] Note that the name Mannon is close to the word mammon which is synonymous with the worship of riches – at the expense of human values.

[4] With the exception of the Blessed or South Sea Isles.

T.S. ELIOT: *Murder in the Cathedral*

More than any other comparatively recent play *Murder in the Cathedral* discusses the question of Fate and personal responsibility. It also reverts to classical times with the use of a Chorus, the women of Canterbury, giving us the background to and commenting on the action, and, although this Chorus does not dance, it speaks in (some pretty wonderful) verse. In addition what the Chorus has to say about the life of the powerless and the abuse of power by those who have it resonates throughout the ages and, for me certainly, especially today. The play warrants and rewards study on many levels.

Murder in the Cathedral was written for the 1935 Canterbury Festival. It was written at the instigation of the Bishop of Chichester, George Bell, who had previously brought together Eliot and the producer E. Martin Browne for Eliot's pageant *The Rock* the previous year. The same team was responsible for *Murder in the Cathedral*. The production was an instant success and transferred to the Mercury Theatre in Notting Hill Gate, playing there for months and was one of the first plays to be broadcast on BBC Television in 1936.

There is an interesting alternative dramatisation of the conflict between Thomas a Becket and King Henry II written by the French playwright Jean Anouilh in 1959. In Eliot's play the conflict between the two protagonists is reported on, not seen, indeed the King does not appear at all; whereas Anouilh focuses on the direct interaction between the two, presenting it as an (almost) one-way love story. Anouilh's play was prompted by an unreliable source, though, so he made the crass error of presenting Becket as a Saxon, whereas he actually was a Norman from near Caen with the family name Becquet. Notwithstanding it is still a worthwhile play[1] and I shall make the occasional contrasting reference to it.

First of all, though, the story of *Murder in the Cathedral*. There are two parts to the play, with an Interlude between them, in which

Becket preaches his Christmas Morning sermon. The Chorus informs us that it is seven years since their Archbishop left, time during which, whether it is rule by the King or barons they "have suffered various oppressions." For them contentment comes with being "left alone." Three priests echo the comments of the Chorus about the absence of Becket and the abuses of temporal power. We learn that Thomas has patched up an unlikely and insecure peace with the King, and is now on his way to Canterbury. When Thomas himself enters we also learn that he feels there will be "little rest in Canterbury/With eager enemies restless about us." Indeed when Thomas landed at Sandwich only the intervention of John, Dean of Salisbury, prevented his being decapitated by waiting nobles. "So for the time we are unmolested," declares Becket. But it is an ominous, brooding Canterbury – the citizens are living in fear and wish Thomas would return to France.

Becket is then confronted by four tempters. The first one reminds him of his youth when he was "gay Tom, Becket of London" when there was laughter and singing and "whispering in chambers." He could return to "kissing time below the stairs", resume his friendship with the King, and thus save his life. "You come twenty years too late," says Thomas. The second tempter offers Thomas "the power and the glory": were he to return to the Chancellorship he would be able to "set down the great, protect the poor." But Thomas will not "descend to desire a punier power": after all, with "power from the Pope", he keeps "the keys of heaven and hell, supreme alone in England." Thus two tempters are rejected.

The third tempter represents "the lords ...(who)...care for the country: we are the backbone of the nation." Claiming that Becket's friendship with the King is over and there being no hope of reconciliation, the Church should unite with the barons: "Church and people have good cause against the throne." But Thomas, as well as knowing the duplicity of the barons, will not betray his King. Thomas finds the fourth, unexpected, tempter, much more difficult to deal with. He claims that Thomas has already chosen his way forward, the way of martyrdom: "make yourself the lowest on earth, to be high in heaven." It is the temptation he fears – that it is his pride which is seeking martyrdom. The four tempters join in a Chorus-like denunciation of worldly accomplishments: "man's life is a cheat and a disappointment." Another chorus of Chorus, Priests and Tempters warn that "death has a hundred hands and walks by a thousand ways." The Chorus is full of despair, feeling that God is leaving them and that if Thomas destroys himself they too will be destroyed. At the end of Part 1 Thomas acknowledges the power of the argument of the fourth tempter – "to do the right deed for the wrong reason" – and he also acknowledges that what remains of his history might seem to be:

"Senseless self-slaughter of a lunatic,
Arrogant passion of a fanatic"

but he nonetheless asks his God-appointed good Angel to guide and guard him.

We then hear the sermon Becket preached on Christmas morning 1170 in his cathedral, Canterbury. He is talking about peace, an inner peace, not a worldly peace. He points out that the day celebrating the birth of Christ is followed by the day of St Stephen, the first martyr. Thus birth and death are conjointly celebrated. At the end of his sermon Becket warns: "I do not think I shall ever preach to you again." He has reconciled himself fully to his martyrdom, for, as he argued, "the true martyr is he who has become the instrument of God, who has lost his will in the will of God, and who no longer desires anything for himself, not even the glory of being a martyr." By becoming this instrument of God, Becket has achieved peace with himself and knows that very soon the people of Canterbury will have "yet another martyr."

Part II of *Murder in the Cathedral* takes place four days later, the 29th December, initially in the Archbishops' hall. The Chorus, as ever in gloomy mood, tells us that "the owl rehearses the hollow note of death." Three priests, carrying successively the banners of St. Stephen, St. John the Apostle and the Holy Innocents, speak of time passing and their fears, concluding that: "Even now, in sordid particulars/The eternal design may appear." Whereupon the four knights enter, claiming that by the King's order they have business with the Archbishop, and placing the business they have to do before the priests' invitation to dinner. When Thomas enters he assures that all his paperwork is now in order and he welcomes the knights "whatever your business may be." In chorus the three knights conclude that Becket is "the man who cheated, swindled, lied; broke his oath and betrayed his King." Thomas claims loyalty to the King, except where holy orders intervene, and, when the knights make to attack Becket, the priests and their attendants interpose themselves. Thomas's ultimate defence is always that he is enacting the "Law of Christ's Church, the judgement of Rome." When the First Knight issues the King's command that "you and your servants depart from this land", Thomas refuses, and, basically, his death is sealed.

Not before, though, the Chorus has told of its "subtle forebodings": "I have smelt them, the death-bringers." And not before Thomas has wished peace on the citizens of Canterbury, saying that what is about to happen will seem like a dream because "human kind cannot bear very much reality." He himself has had "a tremor of bliss, a wink of heaven", and he sees all things proceeding to "a joyful consummation." His priests drag Thomas off to the altar in the cathedral, believing that the knights will not dare to break in, but Thomas orders the doors to be opened. When the knights enter they are slightly tipsy. Thomas's offences are reiterated: wrong excommunications; the need to renounce his episcopal power; appropriating money from the King; violation of due obedience. "Traitor! Traitor! Traitor!" is hurled at Thomas and, commending himself to God and His saints and martyrs, Thomas is stabbed to death. The Chorus then laments that it is not just the city of Canterbury that has been defiled, but that "the world ... is wholly foul."

That, however, is not the end of the play. After the climax of the murder there is a kind of calming, a reduction of the heightened tension, bringing the audience down to a less exciting reality, as the Knights, speaking in prose, rationally explain why Thomas had to die. The claims are made that these are "four plain Englishmen who put our country first"; that violence is at times the only way to achieve social justice, to ensure that the welfare of the state assumes priority over the pretensions of the Church; and that Becket as "a monster of egotism" had determined on his own death so that the verdict on this death has to be "Suicide, while of Unsound Mind." Finally, the Third Priest asserts that the church is fortified by persecution and that "God has given us another Saint in Canterbury." The Chorus, "the scrubbers and sweepers of

Canterbury", agrees: where Thomas's blood has been shed is holy ground and therefore a blessing, thanks to God, has been brought to Canterbury. The play concludes with the Chorus reiterating its fear of the injustice of men and the unexpected violent death, but more than this they fear the love of God – and they ask for mercy and for the Blessed Thomas to "pray for us."

It's a good story well told. And totally grounded in the reality of historical events. It raises again the issue of Fate. Are tragic heroes by their nature moving inevitably towards their death? Driven from within by a particular character trait their life's progress is one towards a sacrificial death. In *Murder in the Cathedral* we are not witness to the excesses of Becket's youth and his close friendship with Henry II, but they have been well documented and Eliot refers to them, so what has changed in Becket? Quite simply he grows: he grows up, he grows into a role and he grows into accepting responsibility. Once he accepted his role as Archbishop of Canterbury he lived that role to the full, just as he had lived life to the full as a young man. The First Priest has alerted us to Thomas's nature of feeling "always insecure … always isolated". Even as Chancellor he loathed "power given by temporal devolution/Wishing subjection to God alone." So his acceptance of Henry's gift of the Archbishopric inevitably led him on a collision course with Henry. Particularly so as the First Priest has already identified pride as an outstanding characteristic of Becket's. As we have seen, Becket is aware of his pride tempting him be a martyr, but has reconciled this by putting himself in the hands of God. He has found peace, but is it based on humility? Does the tragic hero ever experience humility or is it always pride which leads him/her to death? Perhaps humility and pride are sides of the same coin?

After Henry VIII removed England from any jurisdiction and interference from the Roman Catholic Church, the question of whether King or Church rules has been removed from the complexities of government. It was, though, a very real issue of the time. It is neatly summed up by a discussion between Matthew Shardlake and Brother Edwig in C.J.Sansom's novel *Dissolution*[2]: Edwig asks: "And who can hold the k-king to account?" Shardlake replies: "God. He has placed the welfare of his people in the king's hands." Edwig's response is: "But kings have other p-priorities." Of course there is a third party involved in government – the barons, or what we would today call the Establishment[3]. At a time when both the monarchy and the Church of England have very limited power, the power of today's barons remains strong. The Establishment includes the right-wing politicians, the bankers, the City of London, the press barons, the financiers, big business and the top lawyers. Much of today's land ownership has devolved by right of inheritance from mediaeval times too. Indeed farm subsidies, by which landowners are paid by the hectare, amount to wealthy landowners being given £245 by every household in Britain. Of course it is a scandal, but the Establishment, the coterie of wealthy people who run the country, will never confront it.

It was ever thus. As the Chorus of the Women of Canterbury know: "King rules, or barons rule" and to them, the poor have no freedom of action; they can only "wait and …witness." The priesthood too is aware of the abuse of temporal power: it is all about seizing power and keeping it by means of "violence, duplicity and frequent malversation." Plus ça change … The Chorus, which acknowledges itself at the end of the play as "type of the common man", has a good deal about which to complain: "We have had various scandals/We have been afflicted with taxes …/ Some girls have disappeared/Unaccountably." Initially they wish Thomas to return to France, for, as "the small folk drawn into the pattern of fate", they fear the death and doom that he is bringing to Canterbury and the world, and "they do not wish anything to happen." By the end of *Murder in the Cathedral*, though, they thank God for having "given such blessing to Canterbury" for "wherever a martyr has given his blood for the blood of Christ/There is holy ground." Nonetheless on an everyday social level fear abides: "fear the hand at the window, the fire in the thatch, the fist in the tavern, the push into the canal."[4] It is an unjust, frequently lawless society, in which the common man is a helpless pawn. George Osborne's handling of the current British economy underlines how little has changed. Though, having said that, I am glad I was born in England and not in Gaza or the Philippines.

With hurricanes now frequently battering the Philippines the inhabitants could perhaps still fear the wrath of God. And that is one thing that has changed since the twelfth century in England:

the women of Canterbury feared God even more than man in *Murder in the Cathedral* but we have lost that fear. It is interesting that Eliot understood and articulated the misery of the common people. For he himself was very much an Establishment figure. Born in Boston (Massachusetts, not Lincolnshire) in 1888, he was educated at Harvard, the Sorbonne and Merton College, Oxford; he lived in England from 1914 and described himself as "a classicist in literature, royalist in politics and anglo-catholic in religion"; in 1948 he was awarded both the Order of Merit[5] and the Nobel prize for Literature[6]; and, although he was cremated at Golders Green and his ashes taken to East Coker, (the title of the second of his *Four Quartets* and from whence his ancestors emigrated to the United States) he was commemorated by a stone in Poets' Corner in Westminster Abbey in 1967. Yes, very much an Establishment figure, but brilliantly using the Chorus of the women of Canterbury not only to create the death/doom laden atmosphere but also to comment memorably on the unchanging lot of the ordinary citizen.

For his verse is brilliantly memorable. As well as a critic and playwright Eliot is incontrovertibly most highly acclaimed for his poetry. Eliot wrote that "Poetry may make us from time to time a little more aware of the deeper, unnamed feelings which form the substratum of our being, to which we rarely penetrate; for our lives are mostly a constant evasion of our selves." Leaving aside the psychological claim there is no doubt that in *The Waste Land*, the *Four Quartets* and *Murder in the Cathedral* Eliot touches something deep within. In the context of Eliot's critical writings the critic William Empson writes: "(Eliot's) is a very penetrating influence, perhaps not unlike the east wind." That word "penetrate" – that's what Eliot's verse does; it goes deep and is not forgotten. In writing about *Murder in the Cathedral* I have quoted a good deal, so I hope the memorability of Eliot's verse is established, but let me conclude this section with a few lines from early in the play when the Chorus is wishing the Archbishop would return to France:

"Here is no continuing city, here is no abiding stay,
Ill the wind, ill the time, uncertain the profit, certain the danger.
O late late late, late is the time, late too late, and rotten the year;
Evil the wind, and bitter the sea, and grey the sky, grey grey grey.
O Thomas, return, Archbishop; return, return to France."

To conclude. It is interesting to see, briefly, how differently Anouilh treats the same historical material. The one thing the plays have in common is the view that governments keep the common man in check: "the populace must live in fear; it's essential" says Anouilh's Henry II. And then, perhaps, there is the prognostication (and prescience) of the young Becket, "Once the Primate's mitre is on their heads, they grow dizzy with power." Otherwise it is all different. *Becket* is not written in verse. It functions mainly on a psychological level only: we hear the King's lamenting his lost friendship, and the King's past character is established by remarks such as "I had always taken you Highness for a great adolescent lout who cared only for his pleasure" from Folliot, the Bishop of London. Henry II does not appear in Eliot's play. In *Murder in the Cathedral* the action is taut, covering a mere twenty-nine days in December 1190: it focuses on the effect the martyrdom will have on the women of Canterbury and raises serious issues about the nature of Fate and free will; it discusses seriously the relationship between the King, the Barons and the Church – the perennial issue of the uses and abuses of power; and it explores the nature of martyrdom and the temptations of Thomas. "Seriously" is for Eliot an important word. Whereas Anouilh has used history to write a popular play Eliot has used history to explore themes which will always resonate in the human mind. Plus we have, in addition, the verse!

---

[1] A film was made of *Becket* in 1964, starring Peter O'Toole and Richard Burton. Directed by Peter Glenville, there is a memorable scene when the two protagonists confront each other on horseback on a deserted plain.

[2] As the title of this excellent novel suggests, it was set at the time of the dissolution of the monasteries in 1536, the break from Rome having been made in 1534.

[3] Owen Jones's book *The Establishment* is highly recommended reading.

[4] This living in fear is referred to in Anouilh's *Becket* also: Henry II asserts that "The populace must live in fear, it's essential."

Continued...

5 Appointed by the monarch for distinguished services to society, with a maximum number of twenty-four.
6 His *Four Quartets*, which he and most people regard as his outstanding contribution to literature, were published between 1936 and 1942.

BERTOLT BRECHT:
Mother Courage and her Children

In the 1920s Brecht hung notices around the walls of the theatres in which his plays were being performed: "Stop goggling like a lot of Romantics." I suspect that Brecht would object to *Mother Courage and Her Children* being included in these essays on tragedy. For tragedy – the idea of a hero(ine) dying, having heroically given battle to the forces within and without that beset them – is itself a romantic concept. In fact, determined not to make a romantic heroine of Mother Courage, Brecht made a number of alterations to the original text for the second production of the play in East Berlin in 1949, for in the original production in Zurich in 1941, on April 19th, the "bourgeois" press had seen the heroic sacrifices of Mother Courage as being an example of the all-suffering archetypal mother. Unfortunately, despite Brecht's best and expressed intentions, Mother Courage has found a place in the folklore of the loving mother figure, and, as such, has endeared herself to the theatre goer. Maybe it is all a matter of, as D.H. Lawrence had it: "never trust the artist, trust the tale."

Brecht was determinedly non-bourgeois and non-romantic. His was a comfortable bourgeois background, however, with a Protestant Bible-loving mother[1] and a Catholic father who, when Brecht was sixteen, became managing director of the paper mill in which he worked in Augsburg. At school he formed a lifelong friendship with Caspar Neher who set-designed many of Brecht's plays, and the young Brecht on seeing his classmates "swallowed by the army" contrived – by opting for further medical study at Munich University – to experience only the last month of the First World War, which he served as a medial orderly in a VD clinic in his home town.

Almost certainly the political and the cultural background in Germany at the time were more influential than Brecht's personal background. A united Germany (only since 1871) was booming commercially and its values were all money based. Lip service may have been paid to culture, but that was the culture of Wagner, the supreme nationalist romantic and that culture was co-opted to support militarism. Art had become holy. Even after the War, and the resultant unemployment and poverty, there was still powerful establishment forces determined to pursue Germany's military might – and the leaders of the communist opposition to this, Rosa Luxemburg and Karl Liebknecht, were assassinated in 1919. Against this background Brecht first read Marx's *Das Kapital* in 1926. His first full-length play *Baal* had been written in 1918 and his thinking about the purpose of the theatre and life were pretty well formed by then but in Marx he found "the only spectator for my plays I'd ever come across." He also confessed: "When I read Marx's *Capital* I understood my plays."

Well before Brecht read Marx, though, his sympathies with the workers had been expressed in both his plays and poetry. It can be seen too in his appearance, as he had his hair cut in a straight line across his forehead and he wore the clothes of a factory worker. Not for him was the sentimental bullshit of the spate of Expressionist plays that sprung up after the Great War, plays that, after that recent Armageddon, expressed hope through the New Man that was being born, a kind of Superman in touch with the Cosmos. Brecht's plays were realistic, down to earth, as he presented ordinary people confronting age-old dilemmas.

His theories and practical implementation of them were his own, and through initially working as assistant dramaturg at Max Reinhardt's Deutsches Theatre in Berlin in the later 1920s, and then when he returned to East Berlin with the Berliner Ensemble after the Second World War, he continued to clarify and insist on a way of working which we know as Brechtian and which is still a bedrock of much modern theatre.

The principle that is foremost of Brecht's theories is the *Verfremdungseffect*, frequently translated as "alienation effect" but probably best understood as the "distancing effect." By this the audience is asked to encounter the material of the play either for the first time or without any preconceived emotional baggage. Techniques for achieving this included the use of songs to break up the action, actors directly addressing the audience and changing costumes between scenes on stage, harsh or bright lighting, explanatory placards being shown to the audience and so on[2]. It was all to engage the audience not with the emotional lives of individuals within the drama but with the argument, the dialectic, that was being presented. Reason, not emotion, was for Brecht the key to successful drama. He did not wish the audience to feel cathartically purged and thus good about themselves after seeing his plays: he wanted rational discussion to continue and this largely meant the hope that members of the audience would resolve to take action against the social injustices they had witnessed on stage. A towering and worthy goal, with the name Epic Theatre. To some extent Brecht was influenced by traditional Chinese theatre and its style of acting, but for him though the Chinese theatre[3] had a welcome style, it was the substance of his own theatre that was more fundamentally important as he sought "to historicize and address social and political issues."[4]

It is true that Brecht's early plays were written from an anarchist prospective, that from the mid-twenties to the late thirties they were written from a communist perspective, and that subsequently that perspective was then seemingly dropped. But always his plays were written to advance the cause of the underdog, the you and me against the forces of the establishment. So, how is all this relevant to *Mother Courage and Her Children*? The play was written in little more than a month, while Brecht was residing in Sweden, having left Nazi Germany in February 1933, as soon as Hitler took power. Although Brecht claimed that *Mother Courage and Her Children* was written in 1938, it is almost certain that it was written as a response to the outbreak of the Second World War. But it was written as a warning and was written before any major fighting began: "As I wrote I imagined that the playwright's warning voice would be heard from the stages of various great cities, proclaiming that he who would sup with the devil must have a long spoon." The seventeenth-century German writer Grimmelshausen wrote a novel called *The Runagate Courage* in which the main character contrives by hook or by crook to survive the vicissitudes of the Thirty Years' War. From him Brecht took the name of his protagonist and used the same war. The play, though, is owned by Brecht.

Mother Courage and Her Children is episodic in twelve scenes, spanning twelve years. Brecht calls it "A Chronicle of the Thirty Years War." Basically Mother Courage (Anna Fierling) is a trader in food and liquor for soldiers, as such she is a camp follower of either the Protestant or Catholic army, dependent on the fortunes of the war. As she says, "You don't ask trade people their faith but their prices." She – and initially her children too – pulls a cart: "We're doing an honest trade in ham and linen, and we're peaceable folk." Her concern is to get by and to get through the war with her three children intact.

Her first child Eilif, her "dashing clever son" is conscripted by the Recruiting Officer in the first episode, or scene, of the play. He becomes a favourite of a Protestant General who praises him for having killed local peasants and slaughtered their cattle. However, during a brief period of peace, he behaves in the way for which he had previously been praised, kills a peasant's wife, and then is put to death by soldiers.

Her second child, Swiss Cheese, the stupid honest one, gets a job as an army paymaster for the Protestant cause. At a time of Catholic success, (the fortunes of the sides go back and forth) with Mother Courage having suddenly changed therefore to flying a Catholic flag, Swiss Cheese hides the regiment's paybox from the invading Catholics. He is captured and although his mother attempts to barter for his freedom she fails and he is killed. In one of the most poignant scenes of the play Mother Courage, for her own safety, denies having known her own son: "Know him... What, never seen him till he had that meal here."

Katrin, the third child, also has to deny any knowledge of her brother. Verbally that is easy as she is dumb form birth. Mother Courage's brief introductory comment about her is: "The girl's nowt. One good thing, she can't talk." Her mother's hope is to get her a husband once there is a permanent peace settlement. The Cook, a fellow traveller with Mother Courage, inherits an hotel in Utrecht and proposes that he and Mother Courage should leave the wars to manage it, but he scornfully rejects the possibility of Katrin joining them. Mother Courage then stays loyal to her daughter. We have seen Katrin's maternal instinct when, after the Battle of Magdeburg, she rescues a baby –and not for the first time, we are told – from a ruined house. (Somehow Mother Courage has to get rid of such babies.) Her humanity is further shown when with the Catholic forces threatening a surprise attack on the Protestant town of Halle, Katrin, hearing of this, beats her drum more and more aggressively to give the inhabitants of Halle warning. She successfully alerts the citizens but is shot for her pains.

Thus Mother Courage has failed completely in her expressed goal of her children surviving the war. The play ends with Mother Courage tugging her cart along alone, and voices offstage singing:

"Tomorrow is another day…
Wherever life has not died out
It staggers to its feet again."

There are other characters in *Mother Courage and Her Children*, most noticeably the Cook who accompanies the Courage handcart for a number of years and the Chaplain who does the same. By and large they are ciphers, not much more than opportunists both. And there is the army whore Yvette Pottier who eventually shacks up with an ancient Colonel: she does, though, probably save the lives of Mother Courage and Katrin by impressing on them how important it is to deny all knowledge of Swiss Cheese.

The characterisation is not, however, for Brecht, of any great importance: witness the fact that only Mother Courage and her children and Yvette Pottier are given names, the rest are identified by their role or function or job. In his earlier plays he was, using the *Verfremdungseffekt*, persuading us of the objectivity of his approach, presenting material that allows the audience to draw its own conclusions[5]. However with *Mother Courage and Her Children* – together with the other major plays finalised from 1941 to 1947[6] – Brecht is using his distancing techniques to present moral dilemmas for the individual, whether it be to do with science and the church or the family and justice or, in the case of *Mother Courage and Her Children*, war and survival. Epic Theatre is the term often employed to describe these plays and, of course, we the audience are asked to share in the dilemma of the protagonist and by engaging our reason help develop moral principles and a moral position which will then inform all our subsequent thinking and responses to the real world. With both *The Caucasian Chalk Circle* and *Mother Courage and Her Children*, though, Brecht, through his judicious selection of material is very much expressing his viewpoint, with no room for an alternative perspective, on human nature under capitalism[7].

War produces rape and killing. "I'm so scared they won't get through the war," says Mother Courage apropos her children at the start of the play, and, inevitably, she loses all three of them. She has no doubts about who benefits from war: "To go by what the big shots say, they're waging war for almighty God and in the name of everything that's good and lovely. But look closer, they ain't so silly, they're waging it for what they can get. Else little folk like me wouldn't be in it at all." I suppose the counter argument – how beneficial war can be – is briefly presented by the Sergeant in the second speech of the play, when he argues that it "takes a war to restore order. Peacetime, the human race runs wild … Takes a war to get proper nominal rolls and inventories … no order, no war." But this argument is countered by the chaos of the disorderly life that Brecht presents in the rest of the play.

Brecht's view of human nature under capitalism is not a noble one. Commenting on the anger of the Young Soldier who still has got no reward for rescuing the Colonel's horse, Mother Courage pithily comments: "Wanting your reward is good sound sense. Why be a hero otherwise?" She knows that it "takes all sorts to make a world, you scratch my back and I'll scratch yours … You have to cut your coat according to your cloth." You have to make compromises to get by. And that humans are corruptible is a positive: "After all, they ain't wolves, just humans out for money. Corruption in humans is same as compassion in God. Corruption's our only hope."

The only virtue that poor folk have is courage: "Poor folk got to have courage … Mere fact they bring kids into world shows they got courage, 'cause there's no hope for them." Arguably, therefore, the act of copulation becomes vainglorious and foolish. And in the Ninth Scene, after the Cook has broken up the interaction between himself and Mother Courage by directly addressing the audience and announcing a song that he and Mother Courage sing together, we have the longest and most pertinent song in the play, as, stanza by stanza, they sing of the failures and deaths of renowned men, pointing out that it was either wisdom or courage or honesty or unselfishness or fear of God that brought them low and therefore "How fortunate the man with none."

Bravery too is foolishness. Along with what are usually considered to be virtues, as outlined in the song referred to in the previous paragraph, Brecht dismisses bravery in the line: "In decent countries folk don't have to have virtues, the whole lot can be perfectly ordinary, average intelligence, and for all I know cowards." Bravery is irrelevant in normal life, peaceful life. Brecht makes the point that human behaviour under capitalism, in its greed and determination to survive, is the same in war as in peacetime:

> "But what is war but private trading
> That deals in blood instead of boots."

Although *Mother Courage and Her Children* (the full title is so important: so often it is simply referred to by the shorthand of *Mother Courage*) was written, as we have seen, in a fever pitch after the outbreak of the Second World War, it was intended to be seen as a commentary and warning before the acceleration of the war into the horror and slaughter it became. As such, with only the one production – in neutral Zurich – during the war, it failed, though as a universal comment on the nature of war it remains powerfully relevant. What about Brecht's portrayal of the opportunism and cynicism of human nature under capitalism, the overriding sense of selfishness and greed of almost all the characters in the play, including Mother Courage herself? Do we believe his vision?

As already mentioned it is around the portrayal of Mother Courage that dissent abounds. Martin Esslin, in his book *Brecht, a Choice of Evils*, believes that the "real meaning" of Brecht's plays runs counter to what Brecht intended, that the audiences, not only on April 19th 1941 in Zurich, but most subsequent audiences, who saw Mother Courage as "an embodiment of the eternal virtues of the common people" in fact have had the right response to the play: there is something noble and heroic in Mother Courage's determination to survive, come what may. It may depend on the production values of any enactment of *Mother Courage and Her Children* but in any production we have made an epic journey with Mother Courage and it is difficult not to identify with her.

Brecht wrote fifty-four plays and screenplays and a great number of poems. Martin Esslin writes of his "universal validity and appeal to all mankind." Although, deliberately, we are not going to be haunted by the music of the songs in *Mother Courage and Her Children* he, along with Kurt Weill,[8] also wrote the musical plays *The Threepenny Opera*(1928), *Happy End* (1929) and *The Rise and Fall of the City of Mahagonny* (1930) – and *Mack the Knife*, *Surabaya Johnny* and *Moon of Alabama* are songs from the musical plays that, once heard, will forever live in the mind.

Whether or not Brecht's plays fulfilled the manifesto of their author there is no doubting their power, and his theories of dramaturgy are alive and well in contemporary theatre. There is a serious purpose in Brecht's plays, some would say a preaching purpose, but I will finish with words he said when rehearsing his plays with the Berliner Ensemble: "I'm not trying to show that I'm in the right, but to find out whether." Employing various theatrical devices to prompt serious discussion about politics, morality and justice needs, I think, to be celebrated.

---

[1] He once wryly admitted that the strongest literary influence on his work was the Bible.

[2] Examples of this technique abound from Joan Littlewood's production of *Oh What A Lovely War* (1969) and small things like the actors changing their clothes on set in the recent Young Vic production of Tennessee Williams's *A Streetcar Names Desire* (2014).

[3] Other influences on Brecht include Charlie Chaplin's little man, the political cabaret of Karl Valentin and Eisenstein's film *The Battleship Potemkin*.

[4] From *Brecht on Theatre – the Development of an Aesthetic*. Translated and edited by John Willett.

[5] He wants this process, of the audience drawing its own conclusions, to happen individually or communally, via discussion or reflection that has been prompted by the play

[6] *The Life of Galileo* (1943), *The Good Woman of Setzuan* (1943) and *The Caucasian Chalk Circle* (1947)

Continued…

7 We must always add the words "under capitalism" when mentioning human nature: Brecht believed that by changing social circumstances we change how people are.

8 Weill remained a friend and a socialist, but, according to his widow, the great Brecht/Weill interpreter Lotte Lenya, he stopped collaborating with Brecht because he "was unable to set the Communist Manifesto to music."

TENNESSEE WILLIAMS:
A Streetcar Named Desire

A Streetcar Named Desire has a redolently contemporary feel: it deals with domestic violence, homosexuality, rape, insanity, nymphomania and power struggles.[1] All issues that dominate our news and political agenda today. The one area that Tennessee Williams's play does not cover is religious extremism and terrorism; but, of course, in 1947 George W Bush and Tony Blair were not around to poison the world. Yes, 1947. It was both a truly shocking play and a revolutionary one at the time. Audiences loved it: it ran on Broadway from December 3rd 1947 to December 17th 1949 and won the Pulitzer Prize for Drama in 1948. Elia Kazan then directed a memorable film of the play in 1951, in which Marlon Brando[2] brought method acting viscerally to the screen. He had created the part on Broadway and indeed the film had three of the four main actors (Brando, Kim Hunter and Karl Malden) from the stage production; the fourth part, that of the main character, Blanche DuBois, was played by Vivien Leigh, who had played Blanche in the London production. Vivien Leigh won her second best-actress Oscar – the first being for *Gone with the Wind* in 1939 – and Hunter and Malden both won best supporting Oscars. Brando, though, lost out to Humphrey Bogart's portrayal of the gin-drinking river trader Charlie Alnutt in *The African Queen*.

The dynamics of the different relationships, the raw animality of Stanley, the frail and desperate Blanche, the seedy downtown apartment in New Orleans, where the refrains of the street-sellers are *Red Hots* or *Flores para los muertos* – all these aspects of *A Streetcar Named Desire*, they all still work on stage today with electrifying immediacy. In the view of the Production Code, the regulatory censors of films, some aspects of the story were too hot, too "morally repugnant" for a screen audience, so for the film alterations were made to the original play – although a director's cut was released in 1993, restoring all the censored parts. I will clarify what was censored later, but it makes sense to tell the full story first.

Blanche DuBois is the tragic heroine. When her sister ran off to New Orleans to be with Stanley Kowalski, and her parents (and Margaret) died, she was left to manage the already-shrinking and mortgaged family estate of Belle Reve. She herself taught English at the local High School. When the play opens she has taken "a streetcar named Desire, and then transfer(red) to one called cemeteries … and got off at Elysian Fields." She is seeking her sister Stella, who lives with her Polish husband Stanley. Blanche needs refuge, having lost Belle Reve and – she tells us – been given leave of absence by the High School Superintendent on account of her exhaustion and her nerves breaking. The apartment is small, so all three are thrown into close proximity. For Blanche the apartment is "a horrible place", and she sees Stanley as "sub-human" and "a survivor of the Stone Age" – remarks which Stanley overhears.

Stanley is a long-distance lorry driver. He is all male, enjoying drinking, bowling and poker – and sex. And he sweats a good deal. There is no doubt of the sexual bond between him and his wife. Indeed the pregnant Stella laments that she finds it difficult when she has to spend a night without him. Williams says of him: "animal joy in his being is implicit in all his movements and attitudes" and describes him as "the gaudy seed-bearer." Stanley picks quarrels with Blanche, fundamentally about the loss of Belle Reve, about why Blanche has a trunk full of furs and jewellery and about his right, as Stella's husband, to know how exactly the family property came to be lost. He has "acquaintances" who will look into the matter. But he also has an acquaintance who drives through Laurel, the town from which Blanche has fled, from whom he intends to get the truth about Blanche and what really happened in Laurel.

A constant theme, which Williams orchestrates through the playing of polka music, the Varsouviana, is the past marriage that Blanche had to a boy named Allan. They were both very young, and when Blanche caught Alan in a homosexual liaison she taunted him about it, which caused him to go out and shoot himself. She carries the poetry he wrote with her and feels it sullied when Stanley gets his hands on it. Since then she has doubted herself in all relationships, but in the Elysian Fields she finds an ex-army and poker-playing friend of Stanley's, Mitch. Mitch lives with his mother and has an obvious element of decency about him. Blanche and Mitch are attracted to each other and date: it seems possible that each might find a haven in the other.

However, Stanley's acquaintance has returned from Laurel with the truth about Blanche. She has been sacked from her teaching post for having an affair with a seventeen-year-old student; in addition "there was an army camp near Laurel and your sister's was one of the places called 'Out-of-Bounds'"; and she had also been thrown out of the very cheap Flamingo Hotel on account of her immorality. So Blanche's frail veneer of being a gentile Southern lady is brutally stripped off her. She is revealed as a nymphomaniac. It is her birthday too and Stanley has brought her a present: a one-way ticket back to Laurel.

Mitch was due to attend Blanche's birthday celebration, but Blanche has given him an account of Blanche's history, so that when, somewhat drunk, he finds Blanche alone he attempts to force himself on her, saying "You're not clean enough to bring in the house with my mother." Blanche eludes his advances but is driven to hysterically shouting "Fire!" to get rid of him.

What follows is that Stella has been taken to the hospital to begin her labour, leaving Stanley and Blanche alone together in the apartment. Blanche is fantasising about an old admirer of hers, Mr Shep Huntleigh of Dallas, coming to take her away on a cruise. Rightly Stanley does not believe a word of it. Blanche, feeling threatened by Stanley in his brilliant silk pyjamas, calls Western Union ineffectively; she also breaks a bottle in a futile attempt to defend herself. "Oh! So you want some rough house!" cries Stanley. "We've had this date with each other from the beginning." And Stanley rapes Blanche.

The last scene takes place a few weeks later. Stella has had her baby and is packing Blanche's things for her, for, as she tells her neighbour Eunice, Blanche is going on a vacation. Stella explains: "I couldn't believe her story and go on living with Stanley." Blanche fantasies that she is expecting the arrival of Shep Huntleigh, but a Doctor and Nurse have to come to take her away, not without an initial struggle, to a mental institution. Blanche regains her dignity; Mitch rails at Stanley and collapses, sobbing; Blanche leaves on the arm of the Doctor with the immortal words "Whoever you are – I have always depended on the kindness of strangers"; Stella cries out after her sister; and the men resume their card-playing – "the game is seven-card stud."

The main changes that the Production Code insisted on were that there was no explicit reference to Allan Grey's homosexuality: the reason for his suicide was feebly given as a general "weakness". And at the end of the film Stella is seen retreating to her friend Eunice's upstairs apartment, attempting to indicate that Stanley was being punished for raping Blanche by the loss of his wife. Anything other than a superficial reading of the play, though, tells us that when things go wrong in the volatile relationship between Stella and Stanley, she frequently retreats upstairs, but she always returns to Stanley and their differences are resolved in bed.

Blanche DuBois is one of the greatest character creations in twentieth-century drama. She was the last custodian of the Belle Reve family estate and she has lost it. She is clinging on to a fading dignity, and she is horrified by the cramped apartment in which her sister lives and instinctively asks "Stella, you have a maid, don't you?" Her trunk is full of dresses and furs and (costume?) jewellery. She wears jasmine perfume – which she does not expect Stanley to appreciate – retailing at twenty-five dollars an ounce, and contemptuously dismisses the Flamingo Hotel with the words: "The odour of cheap perfume is penetrating." Williams tells us that she is about thirty years of age and the elder sister, but she tells Mitch that it is Stella, in reality five years younger, who is the elder. Blanche is afraid of losing her beauty and appeal: she needs to cover the room lights from their "merciless glare" and Mitch and she have never been out together in broad daylight. In Scene Seven, when Stanley is listing her abuses, she sings "it's only a paper moon ... but it wouldn't be make-believe if you believed in me."

But deep-down Blanche does not possess self-belief. There are two things that have undermined Blanche, both losses. In the first place there is the loss of Belle Reve, and we are reminded of the hereditary weakness of her ancestors when Blanche puts the shrinking of Belle Reve down to their "epic fornications." Blanche clearly inherits some of these predilections. But that is not the main point about her that Williams makes. The loss of Allan, whom she believes was driven to commit suicide by her own insensitivities, is the major cause of her conduct. "After the death of Allan – intimacies – with strangers was all I seemed able to fill my empty heart with," she explains. "People don't see you – *men* don't – don't even admit your existence unless they are making love to you. And you've got to have your existence admitted by someone." Hence her promiscuity, her own "epic fornications" as she entertains soldiers on their way back to the camp after a drunken night out, her one-night stands at the Flamingo Hotel, her seducing teenagers. It is all so plausible.

And Blanche knows that she is acting the part of a lady: she has lost her husband, her family home and estate, her job. She is desperately trying to conceal her other losses – her reputation, her allure. She is hoping to avoid the final loss – of her sanity. The act she is putting on is for others; she claims that "never inside, I didn't lie in my heart." She has been living with failure for years. Sure she has depended on the kindness of strangers, but one imagines she has given much needed comfort and kindness to strangers too. The persona she presents in *A Streetcar Named Desire* is a fragile one, but she is hurting nobody. As she says, apropos Staley, "But some things are not forgivable. Deliberate cruelty is not forgivable."

Almost her last words in the play are "Please don't get up. I'm only passing through." But she makes a dignified exit. It is a multi-layered characterisation that has earned the audience's respect. Blanche DuBois does not simply pass through our minds: she stays there. It is one helluva part to play. Vivien Leigh won an Oscar for her film performance which highlighted Blanche's frailty and fading beauty. The last thread of inner strength which Blanche is desperately and tenuously holding on to was conveyed by Glenn Close at the National Theatre in 2002 and there was an all round splendid piece of acting from Gillian Anderson[3] at the recent Young Vic revival of the play. Those are the three performances I have seen, but it is a very popular play and I am told that it lends itself equally well to black and cross-gendered productions. The performance that critics rave about was by Cate Blanchett with the Sydney Theatre Company in 2009. I would love to have seen that as there were echoes of Blanche in her Oscar-winning playing of Jeanette 'Jasmine' Francis in Woody Allen's 2013 film *Blue Jasmine*, a film which placed two sisters in a central situation and relationship similar to that of Blanche and Stella in *A Streetcar Named Desire*.

Probably coincidentally – for he too has played Stanley Kowalski – Alec Baldwin was cast as Jasmine's husband in *Blue Jasmine*. But it is Marlon Brando who will always be associated with Stanley. Two comparative unknowns, Brando and Jessica Tandy, opened the play on Broadway and received a half hour's applause on the first night. Brando had auditioned for the part at Tennessee Williams's home, where legend has it that he did some house repairs too, and Williams from thence saw Stanley as a younger and more innocent character then he had previously conceived. Brando's portrayal of Stanley, full of raw sexuality and arrogance – thank goodness captured on screen too – brought a memorable tension to every second he was on stage. Looking back Brando was not entirely satisfied with his performance, believing that he had not sufficiently brought out the comedy in the role – and I think it is true of his screen performance when the humour of wondering if Blanche is "a deep-sea diver who brings up sunken treasure … or the champion safe-cracker of all time" and his constant repetitions of "I have a … acquaintance in …" tends to be lost. But it is without any question of doubt an electrifying performance – one which subsequent Stanleys, when compared with Brando, almost inevitably fall short of. Ben Foster at the Young Vic, though, was pretty good.

The admiration that Brando harvested for his portrayal of Stanley, the almost swooning at his muscles and sweaty T-shirt, however, can make us overlook that Stanley was a complete bastard. Williams saw one of his main characteristics as a kind of youthful ignorance and having your wife's elder sister, with her pretensions of grandeur, come to stay in close proximity, undoubtedly makes for problems. But these are the only extenuating circumstances. True, he hears himself labelled "subhuman" and a "Polack", amongst other epithets, by his sister-on-law – and this produces the proud boast "what I am is a one hundred percent American, born and raised in the greatest country on earth and proud as hell of it" – but from the beginning he behaves appallingly towards Blanche. From ravaging her trunk and his insensitivity to Allan's poetry to the final rape, via buying her a one-way ticket back to Laurel as a birthday present, Stanley is – I repeat – a complete bastard. Animal force and sexual strength and prowess are his abiding attributes. "It's gonna be sweet when we can make noise in the night the way we used and get the coloured lights going with nobody's sister behind the curtain to hear us." He is yearning for the one thing he has frustratingly lost with Blanche's arrival. It's all very basically animal and, I believe, no way even begins to explain his insensitivity to Blanche and his refusal to have any understanding of her situation. Maybe he **is** "subhuman."

In what is fundamentally a four-hander the characters of Mitch and Stella are also important. To some extent they are the "straight" people, contrasting with the emotional extremes of Stanley and Blanche: Mitch cares for his ailing mother and seeks (respectable) female companionship, and Stella is concerned for her elder sister but ultimately chooses her husband over her sister. There is nothing surprising about Mitch who conforms to the male norm and wants sex rather than marriage when he learns of Blanche's past, whereas Stella wants – and gets – both sex and marriage. The one thing I find surprising about her, and it is a very minor aspect, is that, amidst the decaying poor section of New Orleans she plays, incongruously, bridge. Stanley's poker-nights and bowling conform very much to the image of the blue-collar working man. I guess the bridge-playing is a hark back to the life Stella experienced in Belle Reve.

Method acting is an aspect of *A Streetcar Named Desire* which warrants a mention. Deriving initially from the work of Constantin Stanislavski with the Moscow Art Theatre (and Chekhov), concerned with finding the character being played within the actor, method acting was developed by Lee Strasberg in his Group Theatre in New York in the 1930s. Elia Kazan, the director of *A Streetcar Named Desire,* trained with him and was a co-founder of the Actors Studio in 1947; he had a profound influence on what Brando brought to the part of Stanley[4]. Tennessee Williams was an admirer of Method actors too. He said of them: "They act from the inside out. They communicate emotions they really feel. They give you a sense of life." Brando in *A Streetcar Named Desire* appears to be doing just this.

Kazan said of Tennessee Williams, "Everything in his life is in his plays, and everything in his plays is in his life." Until his death in 1972 at the age of seventy-two Williams continued to mine his life experiences and write plays. But it is the period between 1944 and 1961 that produced his most memorable plays. *The Glass Menagerie* started it all in 1944; it was followed by *A Streetcar Named Desire* (1947), *The Rose Tattoo* (1951), *Cat on a Hot Tin Roof* (1955), *Suddenly Last Summer* (1958), *Sweet Bird of Youth* (1959) and *The Night of the Iguana* (1961). And Blanche DuBois was certainly not the only memorable tragic figure: Brick in *Cat on a Hot Tin Roof,* Chance *in Sweet Bird of Youth* and the ex-priest Shannon in the *Night of the Iguana* are all splendid tragic creations – and Laura in *The Glass Menagerie* and Catherine in *Suddenly Last Summer* are memorable protagonists too.

What makes Williams such an outstanding playwright? It is his human understanding – of our raw drives, of our sexuality, of our humanity and our frailty, of our despair. When Williams's psychiatrist asked him why he was so full of anger, envy and hate, he accepted the first two adjectives, but not hate. In his Foreword to *Sweet Bird of Youth*, he writes: "I think that hate is a thing, a feeling, that can only exist where there is no understanding." And Williams possesses understanding in spades: so that amid all the foibles and frailties and failures of his characters his love and understanding shine through. There is a splendid recent biography of Tennessee Williams by Jon Lahr, but, it is his plays which have reached out to million of people, that demand to be celebrated.

---

[1] See Harold Pinter's *The Caretaker* for a similar three-way power struggle.

[2] The part was originally offered to John Garfield who turned it down on the grounds that Stanley's was not the main role.

[3] Vanessa Kirby was a strongly convincing Stella in the Young Vic production too.

[4] See Brando's performance in *On the Waterfront* (1951), a film also directed by Elia Kazan.

ARTHUR MILLER: *Death of a Salesman*

My initial thought when I came to writing about *Death of a Salesman* was that here was a play that has become almost a by-word, almost a cliché, for the best of twentieth-century drama and therefore I queried if there were anything more to say about it. But then this selection of essays is about the best tragedies of all time, and then, once you begin to re-study the play, its excellences hit you yet again. J.M. Synge wrote "In a good play every speech should be as fully flavoured as a nut or apple." With Arthur Miller the flavour is one of character: every speech is carefully fashioned/flavoured either to be indicative of or to flesh out the relevant character. It feels like a carefully wrought play. Yet, by Miller's standards it was a play written quickly: whereas he began writing his first successful[1] play *All My Sons* in 1941, six years before it was first staged, he apparently wrote the first Act of *Death of a Salesman* in a day and completed the play in the next six weeks.

Death of a Salesman, directed by Elia Kazan, premiered at the Morosco Theatre in New York on February 10th 1949. It was an immediate success, running for 742 performances and hoovering up, uniquely at the time, all three major theatre awards: the Pulitzer Prize for Drama; the Tony Award for Best Author and the New York Drama Circle Critics Award. The American critic John Glassner hailed it as "undoubtedly the best American play since *A Streetcar Named Desire.*" It has been revived – and revivals have won awards – so many times, but amongst the actors who have played the main part of the salesman Willy Loman are Lee J Cobb (in the original production), Dustin Hoffman (with John Malkovitch as Biff), Rod Steiger (for the BBC in 1966), Warren Mitchell and Philip Seymour Hoffman – and Antony Sher is soon to play it for the Royal Shakespeare Company[2]. I would love to have seen Philip Seymour Hoffman in the part. (And, incidentally, Jayne Mansfield made her first stage appearance – in a very minor role – in *Death of a Salesman*. And it got her noticed by Hollywood.)

Before I tell the story of *Death of a Salesman* I want to refer to Miler's long introductory essay to his *Collected Plays* 1958[3] – dedicated to Marilyn Monroe, to whom he was then married, in a marriage which lasted over five years – in which he sets out his theories of drama and what he is attempting to do in the plays. I will refer to this essay a good deal later on, but for now I am going to allow Miller to explain the thinking behind the stagecraft of *Death of a Salesman*, which also explains why the first title he had for the play was *The Inside of His Head*. Having described the movement in *All My Sons* as linear or eventual in that one fact or incident creates the necessity for the next, he continues: "The *Salesman* image was from the beginning absorbed with the concept that nothing in life comes 'next' but that everything exists together and at the same time within us; that there is no past to be 'brought forward' in a human being, but that he is his past at every moment and that the present is merely that which his past is capable of noticing and smelling and referring to." So within the play set in the present, we see earlier scenes of Willy's brother Ben and of seventeen years earlier when Biff was a football star. They could be called flashbacks, but they are in fact scenes that are ever present in Willy's head.

There are two Acts and a short Requiem in *Death of a Salesman*. Willy Loman, the sixty something husband of Linda, tells his wife that he has returned early from his sales trip: after Yonkers he kept falling asleep at the wheel and waking to find the car on the hard shoulder. He has returned very slowly. Linda points out that he is too old for constant driving, but Willy regards himself as a "vital" and well-remembered salesman "up and down New England." Willy talks to himself a good deal and most of his conversations are with his elder son Biff. At the moment Biff is at home, having been working out of doors in the West. There is constant friction between Willy and Biff, but Willy also constantly harks back to when Biff was a football star, aged seventeen, and there was the real prospect of a successful career in College and football – but he flunked math. And rather than go to summer school to make the grade required, he, according to Willy, "laid down and died like a hammer hit him." We learn that both Biff and Happy are lonely – something incomprehensible and scorned at by Willy. As well as talking to Biff in the days when Biff did a beautiful job of simonising his car and had a collection of admirers, Willy talks to his much older brother Ben, "the only man I ever met who knew the answers." Ben had made a fortune in the diamond mines of Africa by the age of twenty-one and had challenged Willy to do the same: "There's a new continent at your doorstep, William: you could walk out rich." But Willy chose the life of a salesman. We learn that Willy is now only working on a commission basis and is borrowing fifty dollars a week from his next door neighbour Charley. Linda, desperately trying to hold things together, reminds her sons that Willy is a human being and "either ... you pay him respect or you are not to come here." Biff and Happy dream up a scheme of the Loman brothers working together as sportswear salesmen, and to Willy's delight, Biff proposes that next day he visits Bill Oliver, for whom he worked when he left high school, to ask for a loan to set them up in business. The next day Willy is also going to visit his boss Howard, requesting a desk job in New York. Maybe there will be no need for Willy to kill himself by carbon monoxide poisoning, which the tube in the garage has indicated.

It all goes wrong in Act Two. Howard points out that Willy is essentially a road man and he now has no longer any use for him: "I think you need a good long rest, Willy." Howard has not been remotely interested in Willy's outburst explaining what inspired him to become a salesman – Dave Singleton, a salesman still working successfully at the age of eighty-four "and when he died hundreds of salesmen and buyers were at his funeral." In the meantime Happy is waiting in a restaurant, Frank's Chop House, for his father and brother to arrive so they can celebrate together the success of their meetings. Biff comes first and explains that Bill Oliver did not even remember him and that he had been merely a lowly shipping clerk when he worked there for a couple of years. Biff has come to his senses: "we have been talking in a dream for fifteen years." When Willy comes Biff tries to talk realistically to him, but he is not heard and Willy continues to live in his dream world vis-à-vis Biff. The brothers leave Willy behind in the washroom at the restaurant. Then we finally learn why Biff did not try to improve his math grade that summer when, at seventeen, he appeared to have success in the world of American football assured. After he got his result he went to Boston to consult with Willy, who was on the road. He found his father with someone simply called 'The Woman' in his hotel room, and, while Linda was scrimping back home and mending her stockings, he was giving silk stockings to this woman. After this scene from the past is played on stage, Biff determines to leave home and not to return – nor, indeed to write. He has gained a goodly measure of self-understanding (of which much more later). Willy fantasies about all those who will come to his funeral and speeds off into the night, crashing his car and dying, believing that the life insurance money will set Biff up in business.

In the *Requiem* we learn that in fact Linda has paid the last payment on the house that very day and that no one outside the family, apart from his neighbour Charley, came to Willy's funeral. Biff persists that his father had the wrong dream, but it is Charley who has (almost) the last word: "A salesman is got to dream, boy. It comes with the territory."

Willy Loman is – in part – the central tragic figure in *Death of a Salesman*. He constantly dreams: about what might have been his success had he followed his brother's urgings; about the possibility of Biff and Happy making it big in business; about the size of his own funeral – "...that funeral will be massive! They'll come from Maine, Massachusetts, Vermont, New Hampshire ... Rhode Island, New York, New Jersey." In the end Biff goes back West to earn a living with his hands (and suggests that working with his hands would have been the right dream for Willy) and not a soul from his commercial life attends Willy's funeral. On the surface a failure. Yet, rather like Lear dying in the euphoric knowledge that Cordelia loved him after all, Willy goes to his death in the full realisation that Biff loves him. He is still wavering between the two worlds of dreams and hope on one hand and reality on the other, but on an emotional level he has secured the love for which he has been desperately seeking. Writing in the *Introduction* to his *Collected Plays* (1958), Miller dismisses Aristotelian notions of the tragic hero having to fall from a great height and of notions of pride and "an unseen pattern written behind clouds". For Miller what matters is "the intensity, the human passion to surpass his given bounds." And Willy Loman possesses this. He dies for his family, Biff in particular. As Miller writes: "he can prove his existence only by bestowing 'power' on his posterity, a power deriving from the sale of his last asset, himself, for the price of his insurance policy."

Following his brother Ben's advice he goes into the dark jungle, believing he will find a diamond for his family.

In that way Willy Loman is everyman, as in death we leave money for our children, hoping their gratitude will keep us alive, in their memory. As Linda says of her husband: "He's not the finest character that ever lived. But he's a human being, and a terrible thing is happening to him. So attention must be paid."

Linda's role in *Death of a Salesman* is to try to hold the family together, to try to accommodate the needs of everyone. Happy is a straightforward character. Miller immediately informs us that "Sexuality is like a visible colour on him, or a scent that many women have discovered." He is a womaniser and focused on money and will perpetuate his father's dream and hope to become a salesman, though he is only an assistant to the assistant buyer at the local store. He does contribute money to the family, but is largely ignored, even when he makes the claim that he is getting married.

No, it is Biff who matters equally with Willy. It is Biff's tragedy too. Biff see through Happy: "I sense it, you don't give a good goddam about him." But Biff sees his father as "a fine troubled prince … Always for his boys." But by being "always for his boys" Willy has in fact destroyed Biff's life. The all-conquering seventeen-year-old American football hero always had a flaw, of stealing things that were not his: in the present we learn that he has recently spent three months in jail for theft and he stole Oliver's fountain pen: "I stole myself out of every good job since high school." But what his father did was to blow Biff "so full of hot air I never could stand taking orders from anybody!" Right to the end Willy retains this incredible misguided faith in Biff and what he is capable of doing – almost simonising him – and won't face up to the reality of his "dime a dozen son."

Biff and Will do not communicate, do not meet each other with words, but the mutual love is unquestionable. In fact they share a sense of failure, but only Biff can articulate this. Waiting in Oliver's office for hours, Biff is hit by reality – in the first place he was a shipping clerk and not a salesman for Oliver, and so "I realized what a ridiculous lie my whole life has been. We've been talking in a dream for fifteen years." Willy continues to dream through until his death. Not so Biff. He tries telling the truth to his "phony" father and he also goes along with his father's dreams, but either way he cannot get through to him: "Dad, you're never going to see what I am, so what's the use of arguing." He explains that he is not coming home any more, and, exhausted, ends up crying in his father's arms: "To hell with whose fault it is, or anything like that. Let's just wrap it up… There's no spite in it any more."

Had Biff not flunked math, had he not found his father with the woman and the silk stockings, who knows what might have happened to the hero of Ebbet's Field? We know he had a fatal flaw – not keeping his hands off the possessions of others. But the point is he did go to see his father in his hotel room in Boston and much of Biff's life was determined from that moment. He ran away from home and his father's expectations and now, as the play ends, he is the one able to face up to the truth about his father and himself: "you were never anything more than a hard-working drummer who landed in the ash-can like the rest of them" and "I'm a bum."

This coming to terms with himself, while Willy – according to Charley – has never grown up, gives a maturity to Biff, perhaps the maturity of the true tragic hero of *Death of a Salesman*. Certainly this is a family tragedy, albeit somewhat different from the House of Atreus or the House of Mannon tragedies.

Although *Death of a Salesman* is very much a character-based tragedy, it also is a reflection on the American Dream. This concept was articulated and popularised by James Truslow Adams in his 1931 book *Epic of America*: "life should be better and richer and fuller for everyone, with opportunity for each according to ability and achievement." The American Dream offered hope for all aspirant working and middle class Americans. Willy certainly believes he can succeed, as did Dave Singleman, "in the greatest country in the world." But at the core of the American Dream is the belief that anyone can forge a good life and living for himself and his family through graft and hard work,[4] and, although Willy was probably a hard worker, he seemed to emphasise the quality of being likeable above all others, and this quality is not built into any description of the American Dream. Willy's brother Ben took the risks and went into the jungle and came out a rich man: he is much more an example of a man living the American Dream. No, Willy hasn't quite got it. He might exasperate at Biff that "not finding yourself at thirty-four is a disgrace", but then he himself is playing a role, as father and salesman, behind which he is hiding – "I still feel – kind of temporary about myself" he bemoans.

Which leads on to another theme of *Death of a Salesman*: that of abandonment. But before we go there, in the long-term failure of Willy Loman there is an explicit criticism of capitalism: it is a system which uses people and then abandons them when they have no money-producing value. As Howard points out, it's a business world in which Willy has been operating "and everybody's got to pull his own weight." For Willy, though, "you can't eat the orange and throw the peel away – a man is not a piece of fruit." But Howard seems to have little compunction about throwing Willy away.

It is another abandonment for Willy. His father left him to go to Alaska when he was very young, and then his brother Ben left him for Africa. Little wonder, then, that Willy wishes to ground his children with the security of family – both for their sakes and for his. Of course he tries too hard and creates a fantasy world, but in psychological terms it is completely understandable. Ironically Biff, at the end of *Death of a Salesman*, escapes from Brooklyn and sees his future in the more expansive, perhaps symbolic, territory of the West.

Willy's career choice to be a salesman has limited his growth. We are made aware by Miller's directions about the staging of the play that Willy's house is hemmed in from all sides, no room for growth or expansion. He has little success in his sowing of seeds too. For Willy things don't grow. Another comment on his family and his sons. As Linda says, "he's put his whole life into you" but on that level too Willy has been a failure. Seeing his sons as Adonis and Hercules simply adds to his unrealistic expectations.

Yet, does not all this make him Everyman? Wanting security for his wife and children, his family; loving his children almost unbearably and being wounded to the quick by their rejections; knowing that his efforts are not enough and thereby living with the fear of failure; fending off reality with self-deluding dreams and fantasies –

and deep down knowing that this is what you are doing. Miller may have based Willy on his two salesman uncles, Lee Balsam and Manny Newman, but there is a universality about him (and, I would add, Biff) that taps into everyone's empathy. As Linda says "He's not the finest character that ever lived ... he's just a big stupid man to you, but I tell you there's more good in him than in many people." Not a ringing endorsement, but a good enough epitaph for most of us.[5]

Miller's claim is that he is trying to tell the truth rather than write a "tragedy". He acknowledges his debt to Ibsen as Ibsen's plays "reveal the evolutionary quality of life ... to the end the present be comprehended with wholeness." He takes the role of a playwright seriously[6]: he is someone who tries to teach compassion and understanding – which is perhaps the goal of all serious artists. On page 29 of the *Introduction* from which I have been liberally quoting there is a wonderful summary of the images from which *Death of a Salesman* grew. I will conclude by quoting the last "images" paragraph. He is talking of Willy Loman: "Above all, perhaps, the image of a need greater than hunger or sex or thirst, a need to leave a thumbprint somewhere on the world. A need for immortality, and by admitting it, the knowing that one has carefully inscribed one's name on a cake of ice on a hot July day." I am sure that all of us can relate to that and thereby to Willy Loman. And Arthur Miller has left behind a pretty substantial thumbprint, pretty much unaffected by hot July days.

---

[1] Before *All My Sons* Miller had written some twelve plays, mainly for the Federal Theatre Project in New York, which he had chosen to work with rather than take the proffered work with Twentieth Century Fox and Hollywood. Miller was dissatisfied with these plays though one, *The Man Who had All the Luck*, won the Theatre Guild's National Award in 1940.

[2] Written in January 2015.

[3] Miller's *Collected Plays* at the time were: *All My Sons, Death of a Salesman, The Crucible, A Memory of Two Mondays* and *A View from the Bridge*. Probably his best plays.

Continued...

4 Very debatable: Andrews did emphasise ability. You have to possess other qualities to begin with and **then** sweat to develop them. To have the good fortune to be born with a brain, skill or talent is, I believe, not sufficiently appreciated by those who succeed.

5 The American death-row lawyer, Brian Stevenson, memorably has written: "Each of us is more than the worst thing we've ever done."

6 "…I regard the theatre as a serious business, one that makes or should make man more human, which is to say, less alone." (The *Introduction* to his *Collected Plays*)

THE DEATH OF TRAGEDY

It does not feel right to conclude this series of essays on tragedies in the theatre with a play written as long ago as 1947. But search as I have I cannot find a play that satisfies even the rudimentary definition of tragedy, which involves the fall of the protagonist and an experience of suffering and death. We have established that the fall does not have to be from a position of authority or power, but, as Arthur Miller wrote, someone can be a tragic hero "when he is ready to lay down his life …to secure… his sense of personal dignity." And that simply does not seem to happen in modern theatre.

Edward Albee's plays cannot be said to be tragedies. When you think of Stanley in *The Birthday Party*, or indeed any of Pinter's solitaries, the words 'stature' and 'dignity' do not immediately spring to mind. More recently, Helge in *Festen* has neither moral stature nor dignity. Further back in time both John Osborne's Jimmy Porter and Martin Luther are in many ways simply adolescent figures. Tom Stoppard writes memorable plays. Many like the plays of Sarah Kane. Rona Munro's *James Plays*, especially the first and third, were superb, but they were not tragedies.

The plays I have mentioned in the above paragraph could be said to be traditional mainstream plays in so far as they are peopled by recognisable characters. Whereas there is another strand of theatre which could be said to be more contemporary in that it employs characters simply as symbols, although it goes way back to the 1950s and Samuel Beckett. It is the theatre of poetry[1] – with *Waiting for Godot* being the obvious example. Indelibly imprinting an image on the mind of the audience is the aim, whether it be people living in dustbins or up to their necks in sand or Ionesco's chairs or Edward Bond's stoning of a baby. Unforgettable images, but we find no tragic heroes in late twentieth or early twenty-first century theatre.

But are they to be found elsewhere, or is our age so peopled with discredited pygmies that it truly is an unheroic age? Maybe the world of politics is a better hunting ground for tragic figures. (I originally typed 'heroes' but quickly substituted 'figures'.) In the United Kingdom the hubristic Blair and the deeply-flawed Brown spring to mind. In France there is the execrable Dominique Strauss-Kahn. But all are still alive – though I think a scenario in which Tony Blair were found guilty of war crimes and punished accordingly would be the real stuff of tragedy. If we extend our political view further, though, there is a strong case for both Saddam Hussein and Muammar Gaddafi to qualify for tragic hero status. It would be good if a playwright of the quality of David Hare, who very much is concerned with political and social institutions, would turn his hand to portraying an individual on the recent or contemporary political scene.

In the world of films we have historical portraits of people such as Lincoln and Martin Luther King, both of whom I think achieve tragic hero status. I thought for a while, that, on a more imaginative level, maybe westerns produced tragic heroes, and in so far as Shane in the film of the same title and Preacher in Clint Eastwood's *Pale Rider* both arrive from nowhere with a troubled past and, facing their own demons, do some much needed moral cleaning up, achieving a certain stature, they qualify. But then they both survive and, hearing the call of the far away hills, ride off into the sunset where there are "brand new thrills." The adolescent in me responds to such flawed heroic figures, but we can't have happy endings in the world of tragedy!

In fact I saw a film recently which I think qualifies as a tragedy – and like pretty well all the plays I have been writing about has also serious things to say about society. I refer to *Leviathan*, a Russian film directed by Andrei Zvyagintsev, which has won a number of awards including Best Film at the London Film Festival and Best Foreign Language Film at the Golden Globe Awards. It is the story of Kolya, a car mechanic, and his endurance against the odds. The local mayor wants the prime real estate on which Kolya's inherited house is built and Kolya gets an ex-army lawyer friend to come from Moscow to fight the corrupt local mayor. The lawyer has an affair with Kolya's wife, who commits suicide; Kolya's property is bulldozed down by the mayor; Kolya's friends desert him; and he is framed for the death of his wife and given a murderer's fifteen-year jail sentence. All this set in a wonderfully bleak seaport near Murmansk, with the carcass of a whale, a leviathan, on the beach. Music by Philip Glass too. That is a very simple outline of the plot. There is more. Including a satire on the hypocrisy of the Greek Orthodox Church and an alcohol-ridden hunting trip in which portraits of Russian leaders from Brezhnev to Gorbachev are used as targets, but not the more recent leaders – they are being retained until they get "some historical perspective." Every aspect of the film is an unrelenting look at the corruption in politics and the law and the church and at the failure in personal relationships. The burdens for Kolya are heart-rendingly too much to bear. Although the film received 35% funding from Russia's Ministry of Culture, it has, not surprisingly, been badly received by the Russian authorities – for it does show a society and landscape against which the individual's struggle is truly tragic.

Television drama too has claims to portraying human tragedy. In a fascinating article entitled *The Rebirth of Tragedy*, printed in June 2012's *Prospect* magazine, John Gray presents an entirely cogent argument for *The Wire* to be seen as a contemporary tragedy. No longer are we the playthings of the gods but our lives are still prescribed by forces beyond our control. The society in which we live shapes our lives: capitalism works against individual liberty in so far as "the majority of people are more exposed to random events and arbitrary power than before." And this society is something against which man is doomed to struggle, struggle against insuperable odds, and it will bring him down despite the hubris of hope and the struggle for security. Gray quotes one of the writer's of *The Wire*, David Simon: "instead of the old gods, *The Wire* is a Greek tragedy in which the postmodern institutions are the Olympian forces. It's the police department, or the drug economy, or the political structures, or the school administration, or the macroeconomic forces that are throwing the lightning bolts." You can argue that someone like Jimmy McNulty, the flawed self-destructive detective in *The Wire* represents Everyman: our thwarted attempts to live by a code are always defeated by the need to compromise to survive. Yes it is in the world of politics and economics and corrupt institutions (witness world-wide banking) that power resides, a power in the face of which each of us is powerless. It is the stuff of tragedy. And perhaps we need the length of a realistic television drama series, rather than the "two hours traffic of our stage" to portray this.

Perhaps, then, occasionally we will find tragic themes pursued in the cinema and on television. But in the theatre? Of course the death of tragedy has been lamented for centuries. Wagner, some one hundred and seventy years ago, developed his theory of Gesamtkunstwerk (total work of art) as a response to the death of classical tragedy. And later in the nineteenth century Nietzsche explained why tragedy was dead. For him it was this century of rationalism that had killed tragedy; he called it Socratic optimism, the belief that all mysteries are susceptible to rational explanation. What constituted a tragic situation for Nietzsche was an acceptance of the powerlessness of man against a world, and fate, which is cruel and relentless. Real misery is at the heart of human existence: you might get a glimmer of understanding or power, but that makes your subsequent demise more painful and your fall greater. A world in which people prioritise thinking over action is a world in which tragedy cannot exist. Nietzsche cites Hamlet "thus conscience doth make cowards of us all" to demonstrate how knowledge kills action and how tragedy, needing the conflict between Apollo (reason) and Dionysus (ecstasy), was therefore dead.

The great thinkers have had a good deal to say about tragedy – for its links with the human condition and a world-view are obvious. With regard to drama Karl Marx had nothing to say[2], but the other great nineteenth-century thinker certainly did. Sigmund Freud's critical analysis of *Hamlet* is at the heart of his Oedipus complex theory. He claimed that "the beginnings of religion, morals, society and art converge in the Oedipus complex." Tracing back the origins of tragedy via anthropological investigations of ancient societies Freud uses their religious rituals to argue that the passing over of power from one generation to another is, literally, enacted through the totemic meal in which the father, having been murdered, is then devoured by his sons. That ritual has long since passed, but the Oedipal wish to murder one's father has been internalised.

Freud argues that we have advanced from a primitive culture to an advanced one: we now have an awareness of actions and their consequences, which means we now have to face the intolerable burden of guilt. Guilt, for Freud, is introjected aggression, which cultural institutions and the law and then one's super ego attempt to control. The first controller of one's aggression, though, was one's father. So small children have rages against the father – and, in the context of tragedy and its vision of man's struggle against almost overwhelming odds, it should be noted that all monotheistic religions have at their head a Father-figure.

Looking at the world of Aeschylean tragedy Freud points out that it is the gods who preside over moral order: mortals act and the gods punish. The protagonists are simply the sum of their actions and possess no inner world. The plays of Sophocles, mainly via the Oedipus trilogy, move things on somewhat, and there is then a gradual introspective awareness that is developed by tragic heroes. The ancient Gods no longer dwell in the outside world, but now reside within the human psyche[3]: they are there to carry out surveillance and punishment. This super ego also provides us with ideals, of which we inevitably fall short.

I find Freud's analysis compelling. The dark cthonic forces with which we now have to wrestle are within. Copernicus removed us from the centre of the universe, Darwin demonstrated our descent from animals so we had no divine origin and Freud showed us to be the victims of our unconscious desires, over which we have little control. Basically man has lost his dignity and self-esteem, so there is no place for an archetypal tragic hero, somehow asserting his value by his confrontation of powers beyond his control. As Krutch[4] wrote: "We do not write about kings because we do not believe that any man is worthy to be one." Much more in keeping with modern times are our Beckettian characters expressing their response to life, not by action and challenge, but simply by waiting and enduring.

If we accept these arguments there is little place for tragedy in a contemporary world that constantly belittles mankind, giving him no centrality and no significance. In his seminal work *The Death of Tragedy* (1961) George Steiner refers to tragedy dealing with an unfair and ungovernable world, in which things are unrelenting and absurd: it is "that form of art which requires the intolerable burden of God's presence." It is a development of Nietzsche's argument about the death of God and hence the death of tragedy. Yet Freud has shown where the gods now reside so now the absurd, ungovernable nature of life is both without and within. And even if science and scepticism about rationality diminish human significance, man still possesses hubris and aspiration. We strive to be the best we possibly can – and are pretty well guaranteed to fail. There is Sisyphus potential in all of us – which is shown in the theatre of poetry/absurd. But tragic theatre is witness to the gulf between aspiration and failure, between striving for the heights and the descent into the depths. Tension – the conflict between law and lust, between Apollo and Dionysus, between Hegel's example of mutually contradictory causes of loyalty to one's family(Antigone) and obedience to the state (Creon) – is the stuff of drama, and the tension between what we may be and what we are and how this is worked out, as we climb the heights and sink to the depths, remains a potent tension for tragedy. We can be scornful of hubris, willing for the man who exhibits[5] it to be brought down, but we have the free will not to accept the low level of importance that science and rationality impose on us. We do not have to accept a dreary God-forsaken lot or conform to rules of subservience. There is still room in the world and on the stage for tragic heroes.

Yet it is difficult to find a single-person-centred tragedy. Plays such as the 2008 Pullitzer prize winning *August: Orange County* and *The Last of the Haussmans* have their tragic elements, but it is the falling apart of families that is their focus. Perhaps we can learn from two of the playwrights in this collection of essays who have valuable takes on tragedy. Eugene O'Neill writes of the need for the surviving primitive religious instinct to find a meaning in life: the purpose of the playwright is to depict "the transfiguring nobility … in seemingly the most ignoble, debased lives … the glorious tragedy of Man in his glorious self-destructive struggle." And O'Neill, of course, uses Freudian theories in a place originally reserved for Fate or the gods. For Arthur Miller modern man can still be the subject of tragedy, provided he is not ordinary in spirit; he can be a tragic hero "when he is ready to lay down his life … to secure … his personal sense of dignity." Tragedy is optimistic in so far as it demonstrates "the indestructible will of man to achieve his humanity."

I will conclude with the words of Maxwell Anderson[6]. He calls the theatre "a religious institution dedicated to the exaltation of the spirit of man... The theme of tragedy has always been victory in defeat, a man's conquest of himself in the face of annihilation ... The message of tragedy is that men are better than they think they are. This message needs to be said over and over lest the race lose faith in itself entirely."

It is imperative that we hold on to this faith in the theatre, in tragic theatre in particular. The scientific and rational belittling of mankind to be no more than a materialistic money-grubbing selfish scarab beetle has to be resisted. Las Vegas, for example, represents the nadir of man's spiritual aspirations. I am confident that man can rise far beyond the dross of contemporary materialism and tragic theatre will not die. Icarus – and Lazarus – we celebrate you.

---

[1] More commonly known as the Theatre of the Absurd

[2] Marx, though, did comment on tragedy in the context of history, that history repeats itself "the first time as tragedy, the second as farce." (*The Eighteenth Brumaire of Louis Bonaparte*, 1852)

[3] Just as Ibsen wrote about battling with troll folk in the crypts of heart and head, W.H.Auden also wrote of the furies hidden inside ourselves. In his poem *Under Which Lyre* he described the non-stop battle for the human heart between the playful children of Hermes the trickster and the authoritarian children of Apollo the law-giver. He professes a preference for Hermes, while acknowledging that "I have a bit of Apollo in me too."

[4] *The Tragic Fallacy*: Joseph Wood Krutch, 1929.

[5] Signs of hubris are particularly inimical to the English. I well remember the horror of southern Englishmen when the outspoken cricket evaluator (usually of sound judgment), Geoffrey Boycott, evaluated his own skills highly and saw himself as a future England captain. The southern knives were out.

[6] *The Essence of Tragedy*, 1970.

JESUS OF NAZARETH

Jesus of Nazareth was born in Galilee just before the beginning of the first century and died, crucified, some thirty years later. His parents were Joseph the carpenter and Mary. We know that he had at least four brothers – James, Joseph, Simon and Judas – and a number of unnamed sisters. As an infant he probably spent some time in Egypt, escaping Herod's edict to kill all babies under two years of age: we are told this by Matthew and also the Christian father Origen quotes the second century Greek philosopher Celsus to support this.[1] He worked as a carpenter under the tutelage of his father and there are claims, by Justin Martyr, that you could find yokes and ploughs hand-made by Jesus a hundred or so years after his death. There is only one incident recorded, by Luke, of his early life when, at the age of twelve he went along with his family to Jerusalem for the feast of the Passover. Jesus was inadvertently left behind so the family, one day later, had to retrace their steps to Jerusalem and found Jesus in discussion with the doctors of the temple.

All is then silent until Jesus encountered John the Baptist. From then it was all go: Jesus fasted for forty days and nights in the Judaean desert and then began to preach in Judea and Galilee. One of his main methods of preaching was via parables: there are some thirty recorded in the gospels. Those that everyone has heard of almost certainly include the parable of the sower and the reapers, the parable of the talents (vis-à-vis investment), the parable of the compassionate Samaritan, the parable of the prodigal son, the parable of the rich man and the beggar Lazarus. The Sermon on the Mount too sets forth principles that people such as St Augustine, Tolstoy and Gandhi have proclaimed as shining precepts by which to live: the meek, the merciful, the pure in heart and the peacemakers are blessed; we are exhorted to turn the other cheek and to "judge not that ye be not judged." It is all so sensible and compassionate – pacifistic, egalitarian – with a touch of entrepreneurship too.

In addition to his preaching Jesus allegedly worked miracles too: he turned water into wine, but for the most part his miracles were in the sphere of healing for which he never took payment. Examples abound, some thirty-six spread through the four gospels: the blind man of Gethsaida; the paralytic at Capernaum; the woman who had been bleeding for twelve years; the man with dropsy and so on. There are exorcisms too. And there are miracles of nature too, such as his walking on water, his feeding of the five thousand and his curse of the fig tree.

But the miracles highlight the problems we have when discussing the historical Jesus of Nazareth. Most of the information I have used above is taken from the four gospels. Those of Mark, Matthew and Luke (the chronological order in which they were written and known as the synoptic gospels) were written somewhere between thirty and sixty years after the death of Jesus and that of John ten years after that. So historical accuracy cannot be expected and whereas Jesus spoke in Aramaic the gospels are written in Greek. It was important for the gospel writers and for the early church to establish Jesus' reputation as the Messiah; hence the complicated tracing of his ancestry back to David and Abraham in Matthew's gospel; hence the apportioning of a virgin-birth to Jesus (a legend that is central to most folk-heroes); hence the presentation of Jesus' last and fatal Passover visit to Jerusalem as a triumphant ride to death whereas the evidence is that Jesus tried to avoid capture by hiding in the Garden of Gethsemane; hence the dubious story of his resurrection, which Matthew claimed was as a result of an earthquake and also saw the resurrection of "many bodies of the saints." All four writers are focused not so much on history as on giving the early church a theological foundation; John especially, with his emphasis on Jesus as the incarnation of God's eternal Word, is concerned with strengthening the philosophical belief system of Jesus and his followers. The writers of the synoptic gospels were more concerned with demonstrating that Jesus was the Messiah (or Christ), as foretold in the Old Testament, hence the inaccuracy of his being born in Bethlehem. All of which adds doubts to the credibility of their claims about Jesus.

The esteemed Jewish scholar Geza Vermes, in his book *Jesus the Jew*, points out some of the inaccuracies in the gospels vis-à-vis the arrest and trial of Jesus: "Practically every detail of the Synoptic account conflicts both procedurally and substantively with any known Jewish law. No court hearing was legal at night, let alone on the feast of Passover, nor did the words of Jesus amount to blasphemy." Vermes also points out that such was the political unrest in Palestine at the time that "someone could easily lose his life without actually committing any culpable act against the Jewish Law or the Roman state." This, he argues, is why John the Baptist was executed – as "a *potentially* dangerous public figure." And that too was the reason why Jesus was crucified. In a politically volatile period, when crowds had gathered in Jerusalem for a great festival, Jesus had already caused an affray by overturning the tables of the merchants and money-lenders in the commercial sector of the Temple. He had become dangerous and, as Vermes writes, he was handed over "to the cruel representative of a political system which, when faced with the threat of insurrection, often demonstrated outstanding brutality and savagery." This is scholarly argument. The gospels are written with a manifesto-like approach and consequently suffer from a lack of concern for historical accuracy.

Some of the claims made about Jesus are manifest nonsense. Walking on the sea? Then, even (!) more improbable is the Koran's assertion that he made birds out of clay and there is also the legend that he conjured trees not to receive him so he was therefore crucified on a giant cabbage stalk. Judging too by the relics that early church-goers worshipped, he could be said to have had innumerable legs and arms and the alleged splinters from the cross on which he was crucified could probably have built a cattle-shed. Even on a level of mistaken translation there are so many stories to be questioned. His forty days in the wilderness were not spent amongst the wild beasts as Mark says; he is mistranslating the word "hayyot", which more accurately means "heavenly beings" or cherubim.

I do not wish to go further into the discrepancies, inaccuracies and false claims made about Jesus in the New Testament. I certainly do not wish to belittle the powers and magnetism – as evinced by the growth of the Christian church throughout the ages – of Jesus the man. Undoubtedly Jesus not only existed but was also a wise and charismatic preacher.[2] The apostles and his disciples and the way they spread his teachings attest without a scruple of a question to that. But was he the Son of God?

This is where every single doubt I have in my body floods in and is not assuaged by the knowledge of how other religions respond to him. For the Jews there has been no prophet since Malachi and Jesus is a "stumbling block" making "the majority of the world to err and serve a god other than the Lord."[3] However, Islam regards him as a prophet, a mortal who had been chosen by God to spread His message and is mentioned by name twenty-five times in the Koran, more often in fact than Mohammed. Baha'is see Jesus as a prophet and hence a manifestation of God, though, interestingly, whereas the virgin birth and the crucifixion are accepted as real, both the resurrection and the miracles are seen as symbolic. But it is noticeable that no religion disparages his teachings.

Whether we give him the label of Son of God or Messiah there cannot be a greater fall than that of being crucified like a common criminal. In the course of what is mainly a nine or twelve month preaching life in a restricted area he has demonstrated to all eternity his insight and wisdom. This he has given to all mankind. We also share his suffering and his grief. What normally happened at Golgotha, the place of the skulls, was that dead bodies were taken from the cross and their bones were left for dogs to scavenge (which in itself casts doubts about the burial and resurrection of Jesus). In the likelihood of this happening, preceded by the pains and tortures of the cross, Jesus showed immense fortitude in refusing the drink of frankincense, myrrh and vinegar which would have rendered him unconscious, thus ridding him of the agony.

An exemplar to us all then. Oedipus, Faustus, Lear, Samson – none of them had such a great fall nor has had such a universal impact. And, of course, at the last he was contaminated by hubris. He laid no claim to being the Messiah until his final triumphal entrance into Jerusalem: when, before Pilate, the chief priests gave him the title "Son of God" (John, 19, vii) he did not deny that title. But on the cross, about the ninth hour after the crucifixion, Jesus revealed his humanness with the heart-rending cry "Eli, Eli, lama sabacthani?" – "My God, my God, why hast thou forsaken me?" (Matthew 27, xlvi). This was the greatest tragic hero of them all, the essential archetype.

[1] Celsus also suggests that Jesus was in Egypt in later life, in service and learning magic.

[2] There are a few doubters. Nietzsche for one, and Bertrand Russell saw Jesus as vindictive both in his belief in the punishment of eternal hell and in his fury against those who would not listen to him. They, though, are in a minority. Even the self-loving Richard Dawkins, atheist par excellence, acknowledges the teaching and precepts of Jesus as a sound basis for a good-living creed – "a great moral teacher" is how he describes Jesus.

[3] *Mishneh Torah*: Moses Mainomides.

Appendix 1

VIEWS ON TRAGEDY

Some relevant quotations

Tragedy is thus a representation of an action that is worth serious attention, complete in itself and of some amplitude ... by means of pity and fear bringing about the purgation of such emotions. (Aristotle)

A man's character is his fate. (Heraclitus)

Tragedy is the gravest, moralist and most profitable art form. (Milton)

The composition of a tragedy requires testicles. (Voltaire)

For man's greatest offence
Is that he has been born. (Calderon)

One of Edward's mistresses was Jane Shore, who has had a play written about her, but it is a tragedy and therefore not worth reading. (Jane Austen)

The world is a comedy to those that think, a tragedy to those that feel. (Horace Walpole)

The subject of tragedy is the struggle between the outward finite existence and the infinite inward aspirations. Tragedy arises when human aspirations urge us to go beyond the limitations placed upon us by our own human nature and by the forces of nature that surround us. (August Wilhelm von Schlegel)

The purpose of tragedy is the description of the terrible side of life... the wretchedness and misery of mankind, the triumph of wickedness, the scornful mastery of chance, and the irretrievable fall of the just and the innocent. (Schopenhauer)

Sternly, remorselessly, fate guides each of us: only at the beginning, when we're absorbed in details, in all sorts of nonsense, in ourselves, are we unaware of its harsh hand. (Turgenev)

Suffering is the sole origin of consciousness. (Dostoevsky)

There is no coming to consciousness without pain. (Carl Jung)

...in tragic life, God wot
No villain need be. Passion spin the plot –
We're betrayed by what is false within. (George Meredith)

Tragedy would not be tragedy if it were not a painful mystery. (A.C. Bradley)

What makes mankind tragic is not that they are the victims of nature, it is that they are conscious of it ... as soon as you know of your slavery, the pain, the anger, the strife – the tragedy begins. (Joseph Conrad)

Tragedy is like a strong acid – it dissolves away all but the very gold of truth. (D.H. Lawrence)

We begin to live when we have conceived life as a tragedy. (W.B. Yeats)

A tragic situation exists when virtue does not triumph but when it is still felt that man is nobler than the forces that destroy him. (George Orwell)

There is no suffering, no torture anywhere in the world which does not affect our everyday lives ... Today, tragedy is collective. (Albert Camus)

Man is fatefully free and freely fated. (George Schrader)

Tragedy is a sense of life, not a doctrine. It gives account of all the forces, within and without, that make for man's destruction, all that afflicts, mystifies and bears him down, all that he knows as Evil. Aristotle is singularly silent about it, but that is the essence and core of tragedy.
If tragic man felt himself entirely free or entirely determined, he would cease to be tragic. But he is neither – he is, in short, a paradox and mystery "the riddle of the world." (Richard Sewell)

Tragedy lends meaning to an otherwise meaningless doom. (Karl Jaspers)

It is the futility of man's actions which makes him tragic, not his suffering. (Maynard Mack)

Tragedy is more than mere catastrophe. It implies a deeper imbalance between good and evil than just the surface effect of the pure accidental. Tragedy is not simply the horrible; it does not appeal to the purely pathetic; it is not completely terrible or terrifying. Well-meaning people may speak sorrowfully of the tragedy of a train wreck or an accidental drowning; but these are the sudden happenings of chance, determined by an impartial fate such as determines the fall of a coin. A thousand external circumstances may change or speed accidental destruction, while the persons involved are powerless to alter their destinies by will alone. And yet in true tragedy, it is this very will, possessed and directed by the central tragic figure, which makes the irrevocable decision leading to the tragedy, a decision which, once made, is subject to the control of no external agent and is the result of the Achilles Heel or the tragic flaw of the hero's character.

People talk of the tragedy in my plays and call them "sordid", "depressing", "pessimistic", – the word usually applied to anything of a tragic nature. But tragedy, I think, has the meaning the Greeks gave it. To them it brought exaltation, an urge towards life and ever more life. It roused them to deeper spiritual understandings and released them from the petty greeds of everyday existence. When they saw a tragedy on the stage, they felt their own hopes ennobled in art. (Eugene O'Neill)

A tragic hero must be considered a representative of all mankind, an embodiment of some persistent problem in man's nature. (Dorothea Krook)

Tragedy is where hope lies ... Tragedy uplifts and is optimistic about human nature. We experience triumph – we have witnessed human greatness ... Tragedy's one essential is a soul that can feel deeply. A person has within him/her the seeds of his/her own destruction ... Tragic man must confront the abyss ... In tragedy if a hero is destroyed by his own self-assertion, he is nonetheless greater than the people around him. (Walter Kerr)

Appendix 2

EXAMPLES OF THE FATE THEME

The Oresteia is all about the fate of the House of Atreus. Orestes comments:
"At this moment I am like a man
Driving a team of horses and not knowing when
The gallop's going to end."

Chance rules our lives, and the future is all unknown. (Jocasta in *King Oedipus*)

He has insulted me and shall suffer for it. (Aphrodite talking of Hippolytus in Euripides' *Phaedra*)

Long ago a sin was sown. (Theseus in *Phaedra*)

There is a divinity that shapes our ends
Rough-hew them how we will. (Hamlet)

All the perfumes of Arabia will not sweeten this little hand. (Lady Macbeth). And there is the whole presence and impact of the witches.

Wouldst thou hadst been less subject to those stars
That luckless reigned at my nativity. (Annabella in *'Tis Pity She's a Whore*)

Fate, or all the powers,
That guide the motions of immortal souls
Could not prevent me. (Giovanni in *'Tis Pity She's a Whore*)

Just or unjust, alike seem miserable,
For oft alike, both come to evil end. (Chorus in *Samson Agonistes*)

The President of the Immortals, in Aeschylean phrase, had ended his sport with Tess. (Thomas Hardy's *Tess of the d'Urbervilles*)

In *Rigoletto* Count Monterone places a curse on Rigoletto.

In *The Master Builder* Hilda and Solness agree that one cannot choose whom one is going to be fond of, as we are ruled by "the troll within."

"She did come from God!" (de Baudricourt's comment on Joan in *Saint Joan*)

In *Mourning Becomes Electra* the Mannon family is doomed by the family curse – from Grandfather Abe downwards.

There is no escape from the past ... The dead are too strong. (Lavinia)

Strindberg on Miss Julie: she is "the victim of the errors of an age, of circumstances, and of her own deficient constitution, which together form the equivalent of the old-fashioned concept of Fate or Universal Law."

In *A Streetcar Named Desire* Blanche suffers for "the epic fornications of her ancestors" and hereditary nymphomania.

Appendix 3

MORE EXAMPLES OF FACETS OF TRAGEDY

Examples of Flaws or Weaknesses

Samson: trusted Dalila.

Michael Henchard: sold his wife.

Rigoletto: exulting in seduction and the cuckolding of the Duke of Mantua.

Solness: not repairing the gap in the chimney – though this was not the reason for the house fire. And all too ready to be flattered by young women.

Blanche Dubois: needing to keep up pretence as she struggles to maintain her dignity. Nymphomania.

Biff Loman: stealing – unable to keep his hands off the possessions of others.

HUBRIS

Only a very wicked or conceited man,
About to sink somewhere in mid-Atlantic,
Could think Poseidon's frown was meant for him in person,
But it is only human to believe
The little lady of the glacier lake has fallen
In love with the rare bather whom she drowns.

W.H. Auden: Lakes(1952)

Examples of Hubris

I have saved the land from ruin: Oedipus.
I am King and responsible only to myself: Creon.

You will never meet a man more honourable. I here absolve you of my death. Pray that your true born son be like me. (Hippolytus speaks of himself in Euripides' play.)

Til swollen with cunning of a self-deceit,
His waxen wings did mount above his reach. (Marlowe's Faust).

Lear wishes to retain his retinue of a hundred knights.

Not content with being Pope Joan, you must be Caesar and Alexander as well. (Bluebeard on Joan).

Becket is called "a master of egotism" by the four knights, and he himself fears the lure of martyrdom, that he will "do the right deed for the wrong reason."

Examples of Falls from a Height

Oedipus: from all-wise King to a wandering dependent old man.

King Lear: from powerful King to a wandering lonely old man.

Samson: from all-powerful champion of the Israelites to a shorn chained slave of the Philistines.

Michael Henchard: from the Mayor of Casterbridge to a solitary, despised lonely figure.

Hedda Gabler: from a General's daughter to an academic's wife.

Master Builder Solness: a literal fall from a triumphant height to his death.

Blanche DuBois: from ownership of the Belle Reve estate to being thrown out of the disreputable Flamingo Hotel.

Examples of Conflict between Society and the Individual

Agamemnon chose to sacrifice his daughter Iphigenia for the sake of the Greek army.

Sophocles is always questioning the establishment.

"Something is rotten in the state of Denmark", and Hamlet regrets that "ever I was born to set it right."

"You live in a rank pasture here i' the court." (Ferdinand in *The Duchess of Malfi*).

"Must I not do what all men else may, love?" (Giovanni talking of his sister Annabella in *'Tis Pity She's' a Whore*).

Dalila argues that sacrificing Samson was for the public good, which is more important than private pleasure.

Joan resists the authority of the Church and can be seen as "a rock-solid anti-establishment figure."

Chekhov portrays a stasis in society: Trepliov laments "I am in mourning all my life", and Masha comments, "But when I'm married there'll be no time for love."

Miss Julie exemplifies the conflict between the social norms and individual desire/lust.

Examples of Wisdom/Learning (for Audience or Protagonist)

From Sophocles' *Theban Plays*:
We learn when we are old. (Chorus)

No man has ever lived out of the reach
Of misadventure's grasping hand. (Chorus)

It is by the laws of heaven that we must live. (Creon)

And no man can be called happy until the day when he carries
His happiness down to the grave in peace. (Chorus)

From the Phaedra plays:

After all, wisdom is only happening to guess right. (Nurse in Euripides' play)

The fiction that love is a god was created by base lust
Yielding to degradation. (Nurse in Seneca's play)

He who strives on and lives to strive
Can earn redemption still. (Goethe's *Faust*)

For vain pleasure of twenty-four years has Faustus lost eternal joy and felicity. (Marlowe's *Doctor Faustus*)

There is Lear's journey from unthinking tyrant to compassionate human being.

Bosola in *The Duchess of Malfi* changes through experience – from a journeyman spy to a man with a conscience.

What's strength without a double share of wisdom? (Samson in Milton's play)

You have to cut your coat according to your cloth ... Corruption in humans is the same as compassion in God. Corruption's our only hope. (Mother Courage in Brecht's play)

How hopeless it was ever to escape from the class in which I was born. (Jean in *Miss Julie*)

Man's life is a cheat and disappointment. (Chorus of Tempters in *Murder in the Cathedral*)

He's a human being and a terrible thing is happening to him. So attention must be paid. (Linda in *Death of A Salesman*)

Appendix 4

The Protagonists as Archetypes

Orestes and Hamlet: the Avenger

Oedipus: the Child who Usurps his Father in his Mother's Affections

Hippolytus: the Denier of the Flesh

Phaedra: the Lustful Woman

Faust: the selfish Experience Seeker

King Lear: the powerless Old Man

Othello: the Social Outsider

Macbeth: the overweeningly Ambitious Man

The Duchess of Malfi: the powerful Controlling Woman

Giovanni and Annabella: Incestuous Siblings

Samson: the Strong Man destroyed by Woman

Rigoletto: the Lecherous Fool

Michael Henchard: the Flawed Civil Leader

Hedda Gabler: the Bored Society Woman

Solness: the flawed Creative Dreamer

Nina: the Struggling Actress

Lavinia: the Family Agent of Retribution

Mother Courage: the pragmatic Earth Mother

Blanche DuBois: the Faded Beauty

Willy Loman: the Deluded Father

Jesus of Nazareth: the Messiah

Acknowledgements

In addition to the critics and scholars whose books I have referenced, I am grateful to Karen Lewton, potter and Shakespeare expert and to Tom Powell, playwright and Brecht expert. Also among the living, I owe an enormous debt of gratitude to the following actors who, by their skill, have brought me (and thousands of others!) immeasurable pleasure: Julie Christie, Glenda Jackson, Helen Mirren, Carey Mulligan, Jonathan Pryce, Mark Rylance, Fiona Shaw, Patrick Stewart, Mark Strong, Janet Suzman, David Warner and Ben Wishaw.

Also by David Irvin:

Facets of Fear (Raider Press 2010)
Novels for Ed (Grosvenor House Publishing 2012)
Shakespeare for All (Pen Press 2013)

www.ingramcontent.com/pod-product-compliance
Lightning Source LLC
Chambersburg PA
CBHW070657100426
42735CB00039B/2210